COVER to COVER

COVER
to
COVER

Creating and publishing
a print or e-book
in Australia

ANDREW WATSON

radiate

radiate

Radiate Publishing
Melbourne, Australia.

radiatepublishing@gmail.com.au

First published 2021
Second edition 2023 (minor revisions October 2023)
Text © Andrew Watson 2023
Design and typography © Radiate Publishing 2023

Produced and printed in Australia

ISBN 978 0 6487055 7 4 (print)
ISBN 978 0 6487055 8 1 (e-book)

NATIONAL LIBRARY OF AUSTRALIA

A catalogue record for this book is available from the National Library of Australia

Contents

Preface

SO, YOU'VE DECIDED to produce and publish your own book. Congratulations, you've come to the right place! *Cover to Cover* has all the information you need, distilled into one handy volume, using straightforward and non-technical language.

You may have thought about and planned your book over many years or it might be something you've put together recently, perhaps during a pandemic lockdown. You might be thinking of printing a few copies just for family and friends — or perhaps trying for a global bestseller. Whichever it is, *Cover to Cover* will help you achieve your goal.

The book is structured so you can either follow the process from start to finish in the order of the chapters (which are more or less in the sequence of production tasks) or by simply dipping in to whichever bit you need to know about straightaway. The chapters guide you to the next stage in the process and most have an additional section with useful links to websites with more information.

I've spend a lifetime in the book publishing world, working for all kinds of organisations, including government, educational, academic and general trade companies on two continents. I've been responsible for print runs of two million and more, and I've worked on a one-off memoir with just a handful of printed copies — and most things in between. Now, with this guide, I hope you will be able to create and publish something of your own you can be truly proud of.

This revision includes even more information, plus updates to publishing resources and website links. It also corrects typographical and other minor errors and has an expanded Index.

"I love books. I adore everything about them. I love the feel of the pages on my fingertips. They are light enough to carry, yet so heavy with worlds and ideas. I love the sound of the pages flicking against my fingers. Print against fingerprints. Books make people quiet, yet they are so loud."

Nnedi Okorafor, author

CHAPTER 1

Starting at the end

IT MAY SEEM AS THOUGH I'm stating the obvious, but as a self-publisher you must have a clear and realistic idea about your intentions and, importantly, about what your book will eventually look like *before* you begin work on it.

It's sometimes said that everyone has at least one good book in them. Some have a lot more. And some have an idea that extends to a series of related books. Think Jack Ryan or Harry Potter or Winston Churchill's multi-volume *History of the English Speaking Peoples* or the dozens of 'James Patterson' novels.

The book you are planning is likely the end result of a long-held desire to publish something that is important to you — and you alone. It's *your* big idea. It might well have suddenly popped into your head or it could have been percolating away for years. It might be the plot of the next Great Australian Novel or a quest to finally get that family history sorted out and nailed down. Or it could even be a hobby about which you are passionate and you want to pass on your knowledge and enthusiasm to others.

So, whatever led you to the point of wanting to produce a book for the first time, you need to start with a clear idea of what you want it to look like at the end. This is not a project where you just jump in the boat and 'go with the flow' unless you want to capsize somewhere downriver. You need to plan well ahead and to do that properly you need a clear picture in your head about the probable final result.

Ask yourself what you want it to contain and whether it actually *needs* to be printed. Could it be published as an e-book instead? Or perhaps it needs to be both? If you decide you want printed copies, should it be a paperback or does it need a hardcover? Will it be mostly text or do you want to include photos and other kinds of illustrations? If so, how many? And do you need to commission any? Would black and white be acceptable or is it important for all or some of the book to be in full colour?

Possibly the most important question to ask yourself is: *who is it for?* In a commercial sense this would be the **market** for the book. Who is going to buy it? Realistically, why would someone *want* to buy it? And what would be the most useful format for the eventual reader or user of your book?

Give some thought to these basic questions and then take a trip to a bookshop — a full-range bookshop that stocks titles in all shapes and sizes, not just the bestsellers section at Kmart or BigW. Look at the formats that match how you want your book to appear. Note the dimensions and the kinds of materials used. Flick through a suitable book and consider the things you like about it and the things you definitely don't. How would your intended readership react to something similar? Would your target market be inclined to *buy* it?

Visit your local bookstore. Remember to
pack lunch – and buy a book.

Having thought about all that, consider whether books with complex design features might be beyond your technical abilities, especially if you are planning to typeset the book yourself. If you want something fancy, you may have to build in the cost of a professional designer and perhaps allow for extra printing costs for special colours and finishes. And talking about printing, make sure your chosen format is a economical size.

Another consideration will be whether the book is going to be sold by mail order and whether the format and materials might make it extra heavy and thus increase the cost of postage or freight. There's more about this in Chapter 18.

And if you're aiming to produce an e-book as well, it is worth reading Chapter 12 about the different platforms and formats available before going too far. It could be that the magazine-style page layout you're considering needs to have a *fixed* rather than a *flowing* e-book format and this might have implications for how you produce it in the first place.

Once you've got all this nicely tidied away in your head, you can move on to the next stage — scoping out the entire project and then estimating costs.

Title

You need to decide on a title for your book as early as possible in the process. You will certainly get quotes for printing and other elements of production right at the start and it would be good to use the same standard identifier in all later communications.

You may also need to look for some external funding (see also Chapter 3) so you'll definitely need a title on which to hang enquiries, applications and maybe even a presentation to potential funding bodies.

The title itself should not be too obscure. Unfortunately, unless we're talking about a work of fiction that needs an enticing or deliberately enigmatic title, the days of flowery or poetic titles are long gone. Blame *Google*, not me. People who don't see a non-fiction book at a launch or displayed in a shop are more likely to find it via an Internet search, often describing it by the subject rather than by remembering the exact wording of the title. Key words will also help in selling your book on *Amazon* and other online shops — see Chapter 16 for more about this.

A compromise might be to add a slightly longer subtitle that accurately describes the contents. However, in doing so you run the risk of the whole thing becoming too long and cumbersome —

and it could be mistyped or poorly abbreviated when it appears in key databases. This could, in turn, affect searches in online bookstores and other bibliographic databases. There has also been criticism in recent years of subtitles becoming 'mini blurbs' which may actually make it more difficult to search for the right book. In short, try to make it *explanatory* but not too long.

Deciding on a title early on will also help to keep you focussed about the overall subject matter as you plan out the content. Without a clear idea of what the book is actually about, authors can easily become distracted and meander off into the tangental woods and the work never develops a coherent theme. These are also the kind of books that never seem to get finished.

A note about AI

I have assumed throughout this book that you are **not** using any form of artificial intelligence to produce text or artwork. It is, obviously, up to you whether you do or don't, but you should be aware that the book publishing industry currently has serious concerns about AI in terms of copyright infringment (where is the information actually coming from?) and the fact that anything produced in full or part using AI **cannot** be copyrighted.

EXTRA INFO AND LINKS

Some useful advice about choosing a good book title can be found here: https://www.authorlearningcenter.com/publishing/preparation/w/choosing-a-title/2219/tips-for-picking-a-good-book-title-and-sub-title---article.

CHAPTER 2

Scope it out

PLANNING, ESTIMATING, calculating, timetabling, and everything in between...

Hopefully you've already worked out what kind of book you want (see previous chapter) and now you need a map or at least some kind of plan of how you're going to get there. It will include organising the content, calculating the expected costs and working out a schedule that leads to publication. And you will need to consider exactly how you're going to pay for it all.

There's probably a temptation to jump straight to the printing stage — because it's usually the major expense — but there are a few steps before and after this that may cost you some cold, hard cash. You can see most of these in the example checklist in Chapter 23. You might be doing all of these tasks yourself, but if you're not, you need to get quotations for each element. Check the relevant chapters, especially those on editing, design, and printing, for more information.

Planning

So, what's going to be in your book? What will it actually contain? You've had the idea, and hopefully you have noted down the kinds of thing it will include. For many people this can be the most time-consuming stage because it can involve lots of coming and going over your notes, mulling over the overarching theme, deciding which details are important, what information should be left out, and so on. For a novel it might be about developing the plot, deciding on the key protagonists and other characters, describing the settings and locations, the twists and turns of the story, and the ultimate denouement.

I find it useful to start by deciding on the general subject of each chapter, writing them down as a list of headings, then thinking about what each one might contain and listing topics as dot-points within each of them. You will find yourself moving things around as it becomes more and more obvious about what should go where. Additionally, as you proceed, you might decide, as I did while preparing this book, to split some chapters into two and to merge others into one.

You will end up with a list of headings and points that you can turn into subsections and start to flesh out.

What about illustrations? And by this I mean all kinds of illustrative material, including photos and diagrams or maps, not just drawings. Are they there for a purpose or just as an adornment? Will you be able to acquire the ones you want without paying too much in either commission fees or permission charges?

Whatever you do, when you plan out the content, always have a clear idea of your potential audience. It will help keep you focused and avoid personal and unnecessary indulgences that may cost time and money later.

Finalising the content

By this point you should have decided on the format and know enough from planning the content to calculate the total number of pages. To do this, read the section on the order of book in the next chapter and then work out the approximate number of **prelim** pages (including any blanks) the book will need.

Then, to calculate the equivalent number of printed pages containing text, start by counting the words on a text-only page of a book similar to the design you want. It should be one with approximately the same size type, line spacing and column width. It doesn't have to be every word, just the average number of words in five or six lines multiplied by the total number of lines on the page. This will give you an approximate number of words per printed page. Then divide the total word extent in your manuscript by this figure to arrive at the equivalent number of whole text pages.

Follow this by calculating the equivalent number of whole pages containing **illustrations**. You might, for example, want to reproduce some photos at half page size and some full page. Add them up.

Lastly, calculate the number of **endmatter** pages. These will include the index, any endnotes and any bibliography. Add all of these — prelims, text, illustrations, endmatter — to get a total page extent. Bearing in mind that pages are usually printed in multi-page sections, round up the result to the nearest four.

Estimating the total number of pages

Average number of words per line in a similar book = 11

Number of lines on a text-only page of a similar book = 40

Therefore 11 x 40 = average 440 words per page

Say 50,000 words of text ÷ 440 = 114 pages of text (rounded)

+ prelims

+ endmatter

+ equivalent pages of illustrations and photos

= total pages, rounded up to next 4 pages = *[Total estimated extent]*

The market

Now you need to decide on the total number of copies you will order from the printer. To determine a figure, you need to be brutally honest with yourself about the potential market. I have had authors of books try to convince me that their book — and theirs alone — would sell squillions in every English-language country around the world. Even maths books. I have also been in the warehouses of large commercial publishers who made overly optimistic predictions and seen the mountains of unsold and now wildly out-of-date books that will end up in remainder outlets (Chapter 18) or paper recycling facilities or, worse, dumped in landfill sites.

There is, unfortunately, no safe method of predicting sales. Certainly, a large commercial publisher will have a rough idea of the market based on sales of previously published books in the same category, but nearly every title is different and actual sales are effectively the market research for each one.

If you happen to have crowdsourced some funding or even pre-sold copies, you will have a good grasp of the potential market. But be careful you don't extrapolate pre-sales too far. You may have already saturated the market with those very pre-sales and then find that no-one else outside of that market actually wants to buy copies.

One significant advantage of modern digital printing is that you could print just a few copies and then go back for small reprint bites as orders arrive. This is known as **print-on-demand** and for many self-publishers with limited funds it can be a brilliant way forward. See Chapter 15 for more about this.

Estimating costs

So, you've got the content, the format, the number of pages and the print run sorted. But, wait, there's more. Obviously, the cost of producing a book is not just the printing. There are plenty of other start-up expenses such as registering a business name, buying ISBNs, registering as a new publisher, and perhaps arranging for your own PO Box number. (See also the list on page 171) And then you might have to pay for some or all of the following:

Writing Employing a professional copywriter for some marketing material. (Chapter 4)

Illustrations and photographs Commissioning new work or getting permission to reproduce existing images. (Chapter 7)

Editing Employing a professional copyeditor or proofreader. (Chapter 5)

Text design Commissioning a freelancer to design and perhaps typeset the text. (Chapter 8)

Typesetting and layout This might be handled by another freelancer and might also involve preparing or converting the typescript into a format suitable for e-book publication. Even if you do it yourself, you might need to buy some specific **software**. (Chapter 13)

Cover design Commissioning a professional freelance designer. (Chapter 8)

Printing In Australia or overseas; possible upload fees for POD. (Chapter 15)

Shipping/transport Depending on where it is being produced, plus insurance. (Chapter 17)

Warehousing Commercial warehouses may require payment for storing bulk stock upfront. (Chapter 17)

Marketing and Publicity Printing and posting leaflets and press releases, mailing out copies for review or promotion, travel expenses to visit retail outlets, the cost of any book launch, and buying a website domain name. (Chapter 16)

Mail order despatch The cost of physically sending out copies you sell online. This should include packaging material and the actual postage cost. (Chapter 18)

Schedule

I've had authors hand over their manuscript and expect their book to be available the following week. Okay, maybe the week after. I have to remind them that publishing a book is not like writing an article for a newspaper — you cannot expect to see it in print the following day. Apart from huge differences in the number of staff involved in the process, there are many, many variations in the overall processes and all of them are time-consuming with a wide range of very different pathways.

You really do need to be realistic about the amount of time it will take. You need to consider your own availability and take into account your family and work commitments. You might, for example, decide that you can realistically clear two hours a day to work on your book. After a few days you will have a good idea of progress and can calculate the total number of hours the whole project will take. On the other hand, you may want to step up the pace and force yourself to meet pre-determined deadlines, aiming for a fixed publication date.

There are three main phases with sub-tasks in each that you need to build in to your schedule: **pre-production** (planning and preparing the material), **production** (doing the work and getting it printed or uploaded), and **post-production** (distribution, marketing and tidying up everything else). Use the checklist in Chapter 23 to write a list of the tasks and the number of hours you estimate each one will take. From this, knowing your own daily availability, extrapolate the number of weeks and months.

Don't assume all tasks will follow on immediately one after the other — sometimes things need to happen more or less at the same time. And you may need to take a break or go on holiday somewhere in the middle. You also need to allow for time in transit for proofs and other materials as they fly back and forth. And don't assume any freelancers you want to use can start immediately. They won't be sitting around just waiting for your work to arrive, so accept there might be a bit of a delay.

Costs and revenue

Once you're got all the costs to hand and added them up you can spread the total amount over the total number of copies you're planing to print and arrive at a **unit production cost**. Whether you print in one big whack at the start or come back for little digital bites, you're still going to need a total print figure.

Importantly, you need to make a judgement call about the split of sales between copies you will sell directly to customers, and those you will sell through retailers. It's a no-brainer that by selling copies directly you get to keep most of the revenue, whereas commercial retailers will expect a cut of the proceeds by way of a discount. (Chapter 18)

It usually takes some kind of spreadsheet to calculate all the elements and publishers usually have their own way of doing the calculations depending on their specific company policy. For example, some may calculate revenue (and profits) on a per-title basis; others may spread a proportion of the production costs over the first print run and leave the balance to be recovered on subsequent reprints. One large multinational doesn't do any of this — it calculates costs and revenue on its whole annual publishing program rather than title-by-title and routinely pulps 80 to 90 percent of any copies left unsold at the end of each year.

Obviously, if you are only planning to publish a single, one-off title, you can develop your own, perhaps unique, method and it is completely up to you whether you work things out on a per-copy basis or take a global view and just determine total amounts of costs — and the different kinds of income, such as:

- Income from copies expected to sell directly, minus any mailing or delivery costs.

- Income from copies expected to sell through retailers, minus the trade discount they will expect (say 40 to 50 percent for a general interest book) and the cost of freight to their premises.

- Copies with no income (giveaways, review copies, legal deposit etc.)

Funding

How are you going to pay for all this? Where's the cash coming from? If you're planning to use some of your own precious savings, then I strongly recommend you sit down and work out all the major costs before you start. Publishing projects begun by non-professionals can develop a life of their own and drain more money than they ever imagined. Using professionals for any part of the process will inevitably eat up much more than you're likely to have estimated.

Depending on the subject matter, it might be possible to gain some funding from an external source, such as a philanthropic fund or the kind of financial assistance a university department might provide to help a graduate get their thesis published. Some of these organisations may demand 'milestone' reports to ensure their money is being spent productively and some may even ask for a contribution to the fund in the form of royalties if the book is a commercial success. You also need to be aware of deadlines for funding applications — many such bodies have submission rounds that close on certain dates so you really do need to keep up to date and get your act together well in advance.

Another increasingly popular method of raising money is **crowdfunding**, effectively a throwback to an earlier era in which printers would invite potential purchasers to subscribe to a forth-coming book. Getting orders in advance meant the printer could then print exactly the right number of copies without any waste or financial loss. In fact, 'subscribing' or, more commonly 'subbing-in' are terms still used in the industry for pre-publication orders from booksellers.

Doing business

Finally, you will need to consider some of the administrative neccessities of self-publishing. Most of the companies you will deal with during production will require you to have an **Australian Business Number** (**ABN**) even if you choose to *not* register with the **Australian Tax Office** (**ATO**) for **Goods and Services Tax** (**GST**) payments. (See EXTRA INFO below.) And while you could certainly use your own name as the **publisher**, it is advisable to create something different for this purpose, especially if you are planning to produce more than one title. A new business name should be registered with the **Australian Securities and Investments Commission** (**ASIC**). The fee for doing this is currently $39. Banks, post offices and other agencies may ask to see the ASIC certificate if you choose to open an account using that name.

EXTRA INFO AND LINKS

* Non-technical language has been used wherever possible to avoid confusion or befuddlement with some of the more arcane terms used in book publishing. However, if you do come across a strange word or bizarre technical term and need to know its precise meaning, one of these glossaries will help:

  American Association of Publishers: http://www.bookjobs.com/commonly-used-terms.
  Australian Printing Glossary: http://www.kainosprint.com.au/glossary.shtml.
  Writer's Digest: https://www.writersdigest.com/publishing-insights/common-publishing-terms.

* Visit the ATO website for comprehensive information about ABNs, GST, and other potential tax implications: https://www.ato.gov.au/Business/Registration/Work-out-which-registrations-you-need/. To register a business name go to: https://asic.gov.au/for-business/registering-a-business-name/steps-to-register-your-business-name/.

* Useful guide to legal aspects of self-publishing, albeit from an American perspective: *Self-publisher's Legal Handbook*, 2nd edn, by Helen Sedwick, Ten Gallon Press, Santa Rosa, California, USA. (Kindle version also available)

CHAPTER 3

Getting it together

YOU WOULDN'T START to cook a meal using a new, untried recipe unless you had everything you need to hand. The same applies here. You need to check the pantry and fridge to make sure you have *all* the ingredients you might need.

Right now you may be thinking about **writing** the text, but what about the **illustrations** and **photos**? Do you have them? Are they scanned at the optimum level of quality? (Chapters 7 and 15) And have you obtained permission for those items that don't actually belong to you? (Chapter 10) Have you commissioned a designer and heard back from them with a draft layout for approval? Have you double-checked that the websites you mention still exist? These are just few of the issues that may slip past you. In short, do you have *all* of the content ready?

You need to allocate some time to organise and put everything in order — literally. Let's start with a standard order of the component parts of a book.

Order of book

This is, in simple terms, the sequence in which the various sections of the book appear. There are many, shall we say, *unconventional* orderings where some of the parts are omitted or squeezed into odd and unusual places but, generally, you won't want to freak out the reader with too much strangeness.

Despite possible variations, there is a standard **order-of-book** that has proven itself over the years. The sections or chapters in italics are optional — you don't *necessarily* need them:

Prelims

Half title page (blank on reverse)

Dedication

Title page

Imprint page

Contents list

List of illustrations

Foreword (usually by someone other than the author)

Preface (usually by the author)

Acknowledgments (personal, not credits)

Introduction

Main text (usually in chapters)

Endmatter

Appendices

Bibliography

Endnotes

Index

[If not elsewhere: imprint info and any illustration or other acknowlegements and credits]

It is up to you whether all these pages run-on one after the other or whether the first page of a discrete section or chapter — the **chapter opening** — always starts on a new right-hand page irrespective of where the previous chapter ends. For an e-book it is common for sections to flow on without any interruption.

The **prelims** (between the half title page and before the main content) normally have Roman numerals (i, ii, iii) with standard numbering (1, 2, 3) not starting until the first page of the first chapter of the text proper. However, this is increasingly ignored and is almost never done in children's books which often start at page 1 on the very first printed page.

The **title page** itself should always be the first right-hand page (traditionally known as the **recto** with left hand pages called the **verso**). It doesn't have to be *just* text, it can be designed to reflect the cover, if you like, but in any event it must contain the full title, any subtitle, the author's name and the publisher's name. Bookshop staff and librarians refer to this page for the 'official' book title and author name. Sometimes a **half-title** may appear on the very first recto. This normally contains just the book title and nothing else and is usually followed by a blank page (although some authors like to put a *dedication* here rather than adding it to the **acknowledgments**) and then the title page proper.

The **imprint** page immediately follows the title page on the next left-hand page (the recto). It contains the publisher's addresses (postal, web, email), the ISBN, rights and copyright info, the National Library CiP line, any other bibliographic matter, and an acknowledgment of any funding body. There's more about the imprint page in Chapter 11. If for any reason you want a illustrative double-page spread immediately after the title page — often the case in children's and recipe books — the imprint info usually goes on the very last printed page instead.

The **contents** list should include all chapters and their headings. Listing sub-headings as well may be useful when there are long chapters covering several topics.

The **preface**, **foreword**, and **introduction** all serve slightly different purposes. In short, the preface is generally a note from the author about the book, a foreword is usually written by someone else, such as a well-known expert in the same field of study, as a kind of endorsement, and an introduction provides an overview of the content and an indication of the author's intentions. The first chapter could potentially include this kind of introductory material rather than be a separate piece.

The actual content normally starts at chapter one, although there is some debate about whether an introduction without a chapter number can be considered the first bit of real content or if it sits more comfortably in the prelims. This only really matters if you've chosen to use i, ii, iii and so on for the prelims. Anything that comes after the main text is **endmatter** and includes things like the bibliography, appendices, endnotes, and index.

If you have appendices or endnotes and frequently refer to them in the text, consider whether you're just dumping stuff there. If the information in them actually contributes value to the book why isn't it in the body of the text? Does the book need an index? If it does, make sure you read Chapter 6.

Your final materials mini-checklist should look something like this:

Text document Final and complete manuscript, formatted in the correct order of contents and with text styles applied as appropriate with positions of illustrations and photographs indicated.

Text permissions   All text-based reproduction rights obtained.

Imprint page   ISBN(s) obtained and all bibliographic information correct and in place.

Illustrations and photos   All reproduction rights acquired as necessary, and all items scanned and correctly adjusted for formatting.

Estimated costs   Final page extent calculated, quotes confirmed with freelancers and other external suppliers, and updated printing quotes obtained if necessary.

If the total page extent does vary significantly (say more than 10 percent) from the one on which printing and other quotes were based, you will need to go back to your suppliers and get revised ones or adjust the content to compensate. There is no point trying to recalculate on some kind of page pro-rate basis because you won't know how much of the quote includes fixed costs (such as setting up machinery) which don't necessarily relate to the actual number of pages.

EXTRA INFO AND LINKS

For more info about the traditional order of contents and other details about the parts of a book, see Keith Houston's *The Book* (published by W W Norton, 2016).

- Writer's Digest: https://www.writersdigest.com/publishing-insights/common-publishing-terms.

- *Book Production* by Adrian Bullock is the industry standard textbook (published by Routledge [UK], 2012, also available in e-book format.

- The *Style Manual for authors, editors and printers*, (6th edition, 2002, published by John Wiley) has been the official Australian government handbook for all things textual and editorial for several decades. An updated online edition is available but its emphasis is on official governmental reports and especially those being published electronically: https://www.stylemanual.gov.au/format-writing-and-structure/content-formats/reports#order_the_parts_of_the_report. The 2002 print version contains much more useful information about ordering and paginating book components (Chapter 13 in the *Manual*).

"Not long ago I tried to write a story. I got my name and address on the sheet; a title, which stank; and the first sentence: "The stranger appeared in the doorway." Then I had to lie down with a wet cloth on my face."

Dorothy Parker, author

CHAPTER 4

Writing

WRITING A BOOK can be fun but it can also be *very* hard work. Sure, there are those among us who can just sit and magically conjure up coherent sentences and write down everything they want to say in actual, real words, usually in the right order. But, honestly, they are a rarity. In reality, most writing is a long, hard, frustrating slog. Have I put you off yet?

Remember that unnerving fact when you wake at three o'clock early one morning in a cold sweat wondering what on earth you've got yourself into and whether you'll ever finish the wretched thing. But, hey, it's not just you. Plenty of famous writers have had the same thoughts and doubts. But they've persisted — and finally won through.

> *"There is nothing to writing. All you do is sit down at a typewriter and open a vein."*
> Red Smith, sports journalist

Of course, you *might* well be the kind of writer who can just sit down at a keyboard and tap away merrily and it all comes to you as if in a dream and flows nicely and you just keep going and going and going and going until you arrive breathless, just like this sentence but 60,000 words later, at the final full point. Good on you. Go for it. But — and I'm trying to be nice here — that's not normal.

Break it up

There are two main stages that afflict first-time writers. The first is the *it's-all-too-hard* phase. This happens when you start off well but suddenly panic about what a huge task the whole project is and from where you sit right now it looks like it's just too much work and you'll never fit it all in and what about the kids and getting the car serviced or making dinner and how ever will you get the time to write ... and what about ... and...

Relax. Breathe in. Breathe out. The trick here is to break it into manageable chunks. Don't think of it as a whole manuscript of, say, 60,000 words. Think of it as 24 chapters of just 2,500 words each. As far as you're concerned, right now, you're just writing a chapter — about 2,500 words. So, start by writing a list of chapter headings and then under each one write a list of, say, five topics or scenes of 500 words each. 500 words. That's about a page or two of typing. Easy-peasy. So, just start with the first 500 words and go from there. It will add up surprisingly quickly.

> *"Amateurs sit and wait for inspiration, the rest of us just get up and go to work."*
> Stephen King, author

The second is the *waiting-for-inspiration* phase. This is where you stare at a blank screen hoping for a metaphorical bolt of

lightning to hit you so that exactly the right words and sentence structure suddenly pop into your head and you start writing manically until the whole thing is finished. Sorry, but it never really happens like that. This is commonly referred to as **writer's block**. Personally, I think most people actually *do* know what they want to say but they are waiting — probably forever — for exactly the *right* phrase or exactly the right sentence.

Don't do this. It's not poetry. You don't have to struggle endlessly for the right words that encapsulate your true, innermost feelings right now and which then echo on down through eternity. Unless, of course, you *are* writing poetry.

"Write a page a day. It will soon add up."
Harmon Wouk, author

I strongly recommend that you just start writing. Something. Anything. Stream of consciousness stuff. At whatever time of day suits you best — there is no law about this. Even if it's "What I want to write about today is…" or "In this scene, the main character is supposed to…" or "Here I try to describe the way the weather changes from…". You could even write something on your mobile phone while waiting in a supermarket queue.

And then leave it for while. Let it 'rest' at least overnight. Ernest Hemingway said that by doing this, your subconscious would continue to work on it. When you come back to it later, you will have a much clearer idea of what to say and can rewrite and edit as necessary.

An extension of this approach is to pretend you are writing to someone you know, a close friend or perhaps a relative. Try explaining the problem you are having with this section of your book: "I am trying to describe what this situation means to the heroine and how she can resolve it by moving from..." This may help to clarify your thinking and, eventually, the actual wording for that particular passage will evolve.

Whichever way you manage to get something down on your previously blank document, once it is in writing you can start to change and adjust it. However, in whatever way you choose to write, whether you get it all down at the first attempt or keep adjusting drafts, you need to be aware of your *voice* and the need for it to be consistent throughout.

Tone and grammar

Whether they realise it or not, everyone writes in a 'voice.' It might be perpetually angry and assertive or, at the other extreme, passive and lyrical. Unfortunately, writers sometimes drift in and out of one particular voice and manage to irritate readers with abrupt changes in tone simply because they got out of bed in a bad mood one morning and started writing accordingly.

If you think you might be prone to this, you need to re-read some of your previous work and adopt the same tone you were using before — even if it *was* a grumpy mood — to ensure some degree of consistency.

Voice is also important when it comes to grammar. Many people use non-formal and grammatically incorrect language when talking face-to-face and you may want to reflect this in your writing. If so, that's fine and you don't need to worry about the so-called 'rules.' However, *if* it does bother you and you'd rather not have people criticising you for what they perceive as poorly written work, I recommend you head to the excellent and accessible *Grammar Girl* website for guidance. (See EXTRA INFO)

Style

Although it may sound like it, the word *style* in a writing context is not the same as *voice* or *tone*, nor does it refer to the *styles* you should apply to text in a word processing program. Most publishing houses have preferences for the exact spellings and formats they want to be used for certain words and numbers in their books. This is their **style**. They will probably have a **house style guide** that sets out their policy on these and other textual matters. You could borrow from one of these or, if you're happy to start from scratch, you could develop your own list.

Whatever you do, the most important thing is to strive for **consistency**. I cannot stress this enough. There is nothing worse that reading a book where, for example, the Great War of 1914–1918 is referred to in several different and possibly confusing ways. And having different versions will always come across as inconsistent and thus unprofessional.

> *"Some days the words flow, others feel like wading through Suet."*
>
> Ian Rankin, author

At the end of this chapter is a sample house style list. It could form a good starting point for your own list. But please don't just copy it — change the items to your own preferences and add others as you go along.

Once you have started your own list, whenever you come across an unlisted word in your text which has alternative or spellings or capitalisations, note your preference on an alphabetised document (or perhaps a set of index cards) and refer to this when it reappears. This is your **style sheet.** You could even use this list to systematically spell-check the whole manuscript once you've finished.

Another, fairly obvious, method to ensure consistent spelling is to simply use a dictionary. The *Macquarie Dictionary* is highly regarded and generally recommended for this purpose in an Australian context. It keeps up to date with the latest words and variations. You could, of course, opt for the omnipresent *Oxford English Dictionary* but note that some formats (especially the *shorter* and *concise* ones) have different editions for Britain, America, and Australia, with localised spellings.

Edit, edit and then edit again

Bestselling novelist Jeffrey Archer once said that he never sends a new manuscript to his editor until at least the thirteenth draft. Yes, the *thirteenth* draft.

Another example is the original typescript of George Orwell's (in)famous and widely referenced dystopian novel *1984*, complete with his many revisions and changes. As you can see opposite, the first version didn't quite make the grade for him and the opening paragraph that appears in the published book is significantly different from the original draft.

The point is that however famous, well-regarded and experienced an author might be, she or he has probably changed, rewritten and edited and had their work reviewed and changed several times before it got to the typesetting stage.

First draft of 1984 by George Orwell

Academic disassembling

Now a quick word about turning an academic thesis or essay into a published book: don't. Many have tried and plenty have failed. A thesis is an utterly different beast from a commercially published book. To begin with, it is intended for a significantly different primary audience — usually academic examiners. It is designed to prove that you have done the necessary research and formulated a substantive and coherent conclusion.

The thesis itself will, naturally, adhere to the academic convention of an introduction, a body of evidence, and a conclusion, not just for the whole work, but for each chapter within it. In simple terms, you are telling the reader what you going to say, then saying it, and then summarising what you've just said.

Paragraphs will be almost unreadably long, based on the requirement that the relevant information should be presented in context, with evidence. And there will be scores of in-text references and footnotes, and probably a lengthy bibliography, all intended to justify your conclusion.

However, if you have researched a subject extensively and really, really, really feel the need to produce a book about it, my strong recommendation is that you don't try to adjust your thesis but — however painful this sounds — use the information it contains and start writing again from scratch. In this way you can ensure the whole text has a consistent tone and flows smoothly. You can also cut back on references and include only the ones that are absolutely necessary. If there is something in a footnote that *must* go in, consider whether that information should be included in the body of the text itself.

Sure, you could use the same chapter order and general structure and perhaps even list the contents in those dot points I mentioned earlier but, trust me, going to and fro trying to change what is already written is the stuff of nightmares.

I also strongly encourage you to also read the guidance published by Melbourne University Publishing which reinforces everything I'm saying here. The link is in EXTRA INFO at the end of this chapter.

Referencing and notes

Unless you're writing a textbook or an academic book that you expect to be read by fellow scholars — or anyone else you think might be exceptionally picky — there is little need to include extensive referencing. However, if you do feel the need, it is important that any in-text referencing style does not interrupt the flow of the text and confuse the reader. It is probably only necessary to use standard author-date entries (often referred to as Harvard style) to point readers to further details in the bibliography. It would thus appear in the text as (Watson, 2021) which is enough to find the full entry at the back of the book.

> *"I can't get on with footnotes. Having two conversations at once. Or trying to have one, and being constantly interrupted by the bloke with the parmesan."*
>
> Hugh Laurie, actor and writer

Again, if there are footnotes or endnotes which contain important information, ask yourself why such information is not in the actual body of the text. If it is that important, why is it not there instead?

All your own work

Make sure that everything you write and include in your book really is your *own* work. There are strict regulations about copying passages, illustrations or graphics originated by someone else. For more precise details, visit the Copyright Council website and download the relevant information sheets.

EXTRA INFO AND LINKS

- A brilliant way to visualise the planning process with sticky notes: https://www. janefriedman.com/create-a-book-map-for-your-nonfiction-book/.

- *Grammar Girl* lives here: https://www.quickanddirtytips.com/grammar-girl.

- The MUP advice on *Turning Your Thesis into a Book* is here: https://www.mup.com.au/blog/turning-your-thesis-into-a-book. See also *Converting your PhD Thesis into a Book in Five Steps*: https://scientific-publishing.webshop.elsevier.com/manuscript-preparation/converting-phd-thesis-into-book-five-steps/.

- Copyright Council factsheets: https://www.copyright.org.au/browse/book/ACC-An-Introduction-to-Copyright-in-Australia-INFO010.

- Applying formatting styles as you write the text will save time and trouble later on, especially if you're thinking of publishing in both print and e-book formats: https://www.louiseharnbyproofreader.com/blog/formatting-your-book-in-word-how-to-save-time-with-the-styles-tool.

- The *Style Manual* has been the official Australian government handbook for all things textual and editorial for several decades and remains the default guide to notes and referencing (although the emphasis is now firmly on online and electronic publishing). Available online at: https://www.stylemanual.gov.au/.

- The *Chicago Manual of Style* is another highly authoritative guide. (17th edition, 2017, published by Chicago University Press) It is also available online: http://www.chicagomanualofstyle.org/home.html. See also *New Hart's Rules*, mentioned on page 39.

- Some organisations make their house style guides available online:
  BBC: https://www.bbc.co.uk/newsstyleguide.
  Buzzfeed: https://www.buzzfeed.com/emmyf/buzzfeed-style-guide.

Cambridge University Press: https://www.cambridge.org/core/services/aop-file-manager/file/5b32459c966af7d2758ca17a/Elements-author-style-guide-2018.pdf.
Greenslade: A free online style guide produced by an Australian book editor: http://www.editoraustralia.com/styleguide.html.
Museums Victoria: http://www.museumsvictoria.com.au.au/collections-research/journals/memoirs-of-museum-victoria/guidelines-for-authors.
The Economist: https://www.benjaminjameswaddell.com/wp-content/uploads/2018/08/the-economist-style-guide.pdf.
The Guardian: https://www.theguardian.com/guardian-observer-style-guide-a.

❀ This *Guardian* series about writers and how they approach their personal writing days is well worth a visit: https://www.theguardian.com/books/series/my-writing-day. Also see: https://www.theguardian.com/lifeandstyle/2022/dec/30/are-you-bored-yet-maybe-it-is-time-to-write-that-great-novel-here-are-some-tips-to-get-going?

❀ Writer's Centres in Australian provide advice and information on self-publishing and their websites contain links to local groups:

ACT: https://marion.ink/about-marion.
NSW: https://writingnsw.org.au/.
Northern Territory: https://www.ntwriters.com.au.
Queensland: https://queenslandwriters.org.au/.
South Australia: https://writerssa.org.au/.
Tasmania: https://taswriters.org/.
Western Australia: https://www.writingwa.org/.
Victoria: https://writersvictoria.org.au/.

❀ Note that any text produced by artificial intelligence (AI) cannot be copyrighted. There are also concerns that AI software may 'scrape' already copyrighted information and thus infringe existing intellectual property ownership.

SAMPLE HOUSE STYLES

World War One or Two, not I or II, or 1 or 2, and not Second or First World War or the Great War.

-ise rather than -ize suffixes (including organisation and globalisation).

Colour, not color.

Labour, not labor, unless it specifically refers to the Australian Labor Party after 1912 when they officially changed the spelling.

Programme, not program, unless it is a computer program.

Percent, not per cent and always percentage.

No full point after St (Street or Saint), or Mt, or Rd or Mr/Mrs/Ms (because they're contractions not abbreviations).

Numbers should appear without commas up to 9999 and with commas thereafter (10,000).

Spell out numbers up to nine and present them as numerals thereafter.

On the other hand, measurements are nearly always better expressed with numerals for the sake of clarity.

Show dates as day/month/year, with no 'th', 'rd' or 'st' following the day. For example: 23 March 2019, 4 May 2023.

For a parenthetical long dash – (em rule) type two hyphens with one space on both sides; for a short dash (en rule) in a span of numbers (1914–18) use one hyphen with no space on either side. If configured correctly, Apple Pages and Microsoft Word™ will automatically convert these to proper em and en dashes. Many publishers remove the spaces on both sides of an em dash but unless the em really is a long dash in the font you are using, it may look like a hyphen, joining two words together and could lead to confusion.

- Double quote marks for direct quotes, single for everything else.

- End of sentence full points go inside any quote marks ("… there.") unless the sentence ends with a quote within a quote, in which case: " … 'over there'."

- Eclipses must be three full points, and only three, either typed manually with no spaces or with the fixed character set (…) found in most word processing programs.

- Single spaces between initials and no full points. For example: J M Barrie.

- To capitalise or not capitalise certain words is a hugely contentious issue (Prime Minister or prime minister?). I strongly advise you to use a published style guide or manual and follow its advice rigorously rather than messing about.

- Sets of initials should appear without full points (FBI, not F.B.I.).

"If there's a book you want to read, but it hasn't been written yet, then you must write it."
Toni Morrison, writer

CHAPTER 5

Editing

THERE IS NO PRECISE definition of the word 'editor' when it comes to book publishing. Indeed, if you ask a dozen professional book editors what it is they do, exactly, you'll probably get 12 different answers. There's even a book (*What Editors Do* by Peter Ginna*)* that attempts to answer this very question.

The problem arises because there is such a huge range of tasks 'editors' undertake or manage. Editing can be structural (moving chunks of text around to better effect), or deleting repetitious passages, or suggesting additions and major revisions, or it can be straightforward copyediting in which an editor will check for spelling and typographic errors and attempt to improve poor grammar. To cloud the issue, many proofreaders also refer to themselves as 'editors' while some publishing houses have 'commissioning editors' who don't do any editing as such!

For someone publishing their own book for the first time, and perhaps doing their own editing or proofreading, the most important thing is to ensure there is *consistency* throughout the entire text. This cannot be stressed highly enough. Obvious inconsistencies reduce the confidence readers have in the work they are reading. This applies especially to spellings and the way certain things are presented. So, decide on how something should appear, and then when you are self-editing, check that all occurrences of the previously determined word or term are indeed correct.

In order to do this efficiently, editors normally maintain a **style sheet** while they are editing. I mentioned this in the previous chapter and it can be anything from a single sheet of paper to a set of index cards or a computer spreadsheet with multiple columns. Whichever method you choose, it should contain an alphabetical list of words and styles that you can refer to whenever particular words or terms appear.

> *"A series of instincts, thousands of tiny adjust--ments, hundreds of drafts."*
> George Saunders, author

There is no harm in re-checking once you have been through and made the first set of corrections. Errors can sometimes creep in unexpectedly simply because changing something small, such as a spelling, can adversely affect something else later on, such as word spacing or hyphenation, and the way lines and paragraphs turn over onto the next and subsequent pages.

Proofreading

It is always useful to have a second or even third pair of eyes look over your work. Even the most diligent of us will miss fairly obvious things for all kinds of reasons such as over-familiarity with the text, or reading too too fast and not noticing repeated words, for for example. Having someone else scan through it may also help avoid other unanticipated legal issues down the track — giving your 'opinion' might be seen by others as libelous or defamatory. Some people find it better to proofread a hard copy printout of the work, rather than stare at a screen, especially if there is a need to jump back and forth to check things.

Professional editing

If you decide that the editing or proofreading process is above and beyond your personal skill level or you simply do not feel confident enough to get it absolutely right, you may wish to employ a professional freelance editor.

The Australian Institute of Professional Editors maintains a directory (see EXTRA INFO below) where you can search for the most appropriate editor for your book. It is worth noting that the fees charged by freelance editors are normally based on an hourly rate which may increase depending on their level of experience and/ or specialism. You should, therefore, carefully consider whether a more experienced or specialist editor, perhaps charging a higher hourly rate, might finish the job faster and more efficiently and not be any more expensive overall.

Generally, freelance editors will want to look over the job and discuss any special requirements before giving you a quote. Any figure they quote is, of course, always subject to change as they work their way through the text. If you want them to be involved at the proofreading stage or with other parts of the process, such as briefing illustrators, they will, naturally, charge more.

EXTRA INFO AND LINKS

- *What Editors Do*, by Peter Ginna, published by Chicago University Press, 2017.

- The Australian Institute of Professional Editors directory is here: http://www.iped-editors.org/Find_an_editor/.

- The *Australian Editing Handbook* by Elizabeth Flann, Beryl Hill and Lan Wang (3rd edition, 2014, published by Wiley) is the 'bible' of editing practice and contains more information than you ever thought possible.

- Another comprehensive guide, albeit from an American perspective, is *The Copyeditor's Handbook: A Guide for Book Publishing and Corporate Communications*, by Amy Einsohn and Marilyn Schwartz (4th edition, 2019, published by University of California Press).

- The *New Hart's Rules: The Oxford Style Guide* (2nd edition, 2014) is the latest iteration of the Oxford University Press style guide first published more than 100 years ago. It has been used mostly by editors and typesetters and was originally subtitled *Rules for Compositors and Readers*.

CHAPTER 6

Indexing

DOES YOUR BOOK need an index? Obviously, the answer will be *no* if it's a novel. For a general non-fiction title, readers might be able to find what they are looking for by using the contents list or by skimming through the whole text if there's only a few pages. But, if you feel you do need one, here are the necessary steps.

First, you must wait until you have finished formatting all the pages and they are fixed in their final position, then read through the whole book. You could proofread at the same time. As you go, highlight all the words you want to include in the index and list them in a separate file in alphabetical order, adding page numbers as necessary. (In the pre-digital era each word would be entered on an card and the page number added when the indexer came across that word again.)

Some computer programs will allow you to tag words or automatically compile an index but this will only produce a list of individual words (and probably *every* occurrence of that word) not themes, so some manual intervention will still be necessary to produce a usable index. And words may not necessarily be in the same place in the final paged version.

As you go through, think carefully about what the *reader* will want to find in your book. An index doesn't have to contain every single noun, only the subjects about which they will actually be interested, and then only the meaningful mention of that subject, not an irrelevant passing inclusion.

Bear in mind that readers may not necessarily look for a specific word — they may want a *theme* instead. For example, while you might include *apples*, *pears* and *bananas* as individual entries, readers could also be looking for *fruit*. But don't overdo it: if your whole book is about a specific naval battle, there is no need to include an entry for just that battle. Nor is there any need to index footnotes, endnotes or appendices because readers will be led to them via mentions in the main body of the text anyway. And don't bother about things in the prelims or endmatter, like a preface or the bibliography, just focus on the main content.

Index style

Punctuation in index entries should be minimal. The aim is to save space. Use one or two spaces between the entry and the page number. Subentries should be separated by a semicolon.

To avoid any confusion, show page numbers in full: 154–157, not 154–57. Where there is a discussion about something that starts on one page and continues onto the next, the format should be 155–156 and not 155, 156 which indicates a different discussion, albeit on the same subject, but on the next page. Don't use full stops at the end of each entry.

Alphabetise strictly, surnames first. Treat 'St' as if it was fully spelled out as 'Saint' but index 'Mc' exactly as that and not as 'Mac.' Use brackets to enclose dates to avoid confusion with page numbers.

This sample index shows the elements I've just mentioned:

Antidisestablishmentarianism: Church of England 34;
    unnecessarily long word 459

cricket, just not 29–32

dad jokes 45–50

insults: amusing 57; abusive 85, 96–97

operational integrity 89–91, 179, 185

MacBeth, Hamish 78

McCoy, the real 23, 27

St Andrew's: cathedral 669; cross 678; university 453.
    See also St Peter

Great War, The [1914–1918] see World War 1

EXTRA INFO AND LINKS

- The *Chicago Manual of Style* (17th edition, 2017, published by Chicago University Press) has extensive guidance on indexing. It is also available online. The chapter on indexing is here: https://www.chicagomanualofstyle.org/book/ed17/part3/ch16/toc.html.

- Does an e-book need an index? Good question, glad you asked: https://www.bookbusinessmag.com/post/lost-art-index-ebooks/.

Illustrations & photos

IT GOES ALMOST without saying that including illustrations such as drawings, sketches, diagrams, charts or maps in your book will enhance its appearance and at the same time help readers clearly understand potentially difficult ideas or concepts. They also provide visual interest and serve to break the often monotonous flow of text through the book.

However, not everyone is an accomplished artist, graphic designer, cartographer or photographer, so it is likely that you will need to source the items you need from elsewhere. There's a huge temptation to just pinch them for free from somewhere on the Internet — but doing so may lead to all kinds of problems (especially in terms of copyright) and the possible payment of reproduction fees.

The easiest and safest way to obtain an illustration or photograph is to buy whatever you need from an agency or photo library. You can look up libraries directly (see EXTRA INFO) and browse through their selection or look for what you want using key words in *Google Images* and follow the links to the original source. The fee you pay may be for a one-off use for a specific purpose or, rarely, a completely royalty-free licence for any use. Always check the fine print to confirm what you're paying for.

Some image libraries (and this applies especially to state and national libraries and galleries with digitalised collections) may ask about the intended market for the book and potential print run. Sometimes they will reduce the fee if the photos are going to be used for purely educational purposes rather than for a general consumer market.

If you do decide to commission someone else to take a photo or prepare an illustration, you will need to find a suitable freelancer, usually by viewing their previous work online, then briefing them precisely, getting a quote and paying their fee on completion. Some may ask for a form of 'deposit' before they begin work — anything between 25 percent and 50 percent of the total quote. You will also need to make sure they provide the final product in the correct format (I'll come to this later) and there should be a provision for paying a smaller amount (a 'kill fee') if you don't actually get what you asked for.

Importantly, you must establish who owns the **copyright** in the work. The artist, designer or photographer will continue to own it unless there is something in writing transferring all the rights, or at least granting you a licence for a specific use. You will also need to ensure that if the work includes an identifiable image of someone, that person has signed an official release form giving permission for publication. This is a murky area of law given that in certain circumstances photos which can be defined as 'news' don't need such permission, so it would be worth checking the relevant Copyright Council *Factsheet* to satisfy yourself that you're doing the right thing. (See EXTRA INFO)

You should also check that the physical object in an image you are planning to reproduce is not itself constrained by some kind of intellectual property issue. This sometimes applies to buildings and heritage sites such as Uluru, for example, where the Aboriginal custodians have requested that photographs not be taken of certain parts of the rock and surrounds, and the Sydney Opera House, where the governing body do not like images of the building to be used for commercial purposes. (See EXTRA INFO).

Quality

In whatever way you obtain your images, they must be good enough to reproduce. This may seem like a no-brainer but many photos, especially older prints and those in full colour, do not reproduce well after they have been through a scanning process to digitise them. The contrast in old black and white photos can be poor and when an image is converted into pixels it loses definition with the result being no more than a grey fog.

It can be even worse with colour images: when they are converted to black and white some colours (esp. red) become cloudy shades of grey that appear to merge, giving poor definition and making them look blurry. This is also worth noting if you are taking your own photos. For example, a background of mixed shrubs and bushes may reproduce as a grey cloud. This happens frequently with photos of old paintings which themselves tend to be fairly dark due to ageing and fading. You could, of course, adjust the exposure level or contrast in an editing program like

Photoshop but in doing so you run the opposite risk of 'bleaching out' some of the image and, again, losing detail.

Photos taken from old newspaper clippings present yet another set of problems. Generally they will have already been broken up into a sea of dots during the original printing process. You can see these dots if you look very closely with a magnifying glass. They are usually well spaced out to compensate for the 'ink spread' that occurs during printing, especially on highly absorbent 'newsprint' paper. If the dots were any closer they would bleed into a black-grey sludge and render reproduction pointless. If such images are then re-scanned for digital reproduction, the software will again break-down the image into dots or pixels and the result will be a wavy pattern across the photo. This is the **moiré** effect. Care needs to be taken when scanning to counteract this in some way, perhaps by reducing the dpi (see below) of the final image. It can also occur when you take an external photo of a low resolution televsion or computer screen.

Photos from old newspapers may not give you the desired result. Here, Bob Dylan is almost unrecognisable.

Reproduction

Now you've got your images, the next task is to ensure they are all scanned and saved as **JPEG** (Joint Photographic Experts Group, sometimes abbreviated to just JPG) or **TIFF** (Tagged Image File Format) files. TIFFs (and unprocessed **RAW** images) are often used by professional photographers because they consider them better and more robust but many printers won't accept them because they are much too large and data-heavy and they need to be converted to JPEGs before being positioned on the page.

In addition, all your images need to be saved at the correct **dpi**. This refers to *dots per inch* or, more accurately, *pixels per inch*. The dpi determines the resolution of the image. The dpi spectrum ranges from high resolution (**hi-res**) to low (**low-res**).

Printers usually have their own specific requirements for dpi and it is always best to check with them before scanning photos. While older scans can be adjusted downwards (usually re-copied with a lower dpi and the file size made smaller), low-res scans cannot be made higher. Generally, images for a printed book need to be around 300 dpi for satisfactory reproduction. Indeed, some printers will not accept images higher than 400 dpi in case they overload their system. Websites and e-books work well (and load faster) with much lower dpi levels, even down to around 75 dpi. The task of putting photos into position on the page is covered in Chapter 13 on typesetting & formatting.

Photo-editing

Photos that aren't exactly right for one reason or another, especially older ones scratched or damaged can often be adjusted and touched-up or repaired with a photo-editing application. The industry standard is Adobe **Photoshop** but you could instead try the image editing software attached to the photo library on your computer. These are becoming increasingly sophisticated but can still be subject to minor glitches so you should check that any changes you've made have actually taken effect on the final saved version of the image.

Further, any kind of adjusting or editing of the image may increase the digital size of that particular photo file and you may need to re-save it at a smaller size, otherwise you run the risk of it being too large and unwieldy for placement when you come to make up the typeset pages. You should always keep a copy of the original image in a separate folder just in case something does indeed go wrong.

If you are using a image supplied by an agency or library there are usually restrictions about editing or cropping the image to a different size or shape. For example, many art galleries, to respect the work of the artist, will only allow the whole painting to be reproduced, never a portion or extract. Anddditionally, there are often restrictions on overlaying type or other images.

EXTRA INFO AND LINKS

- The Australian Copyright Council has a *Factsheet* dealing specifically with copyright in photographs: http://www.copyright.org.au/browse/book/ACC-Photographers-&-Copyright.INFO11.

- The *Creative Bloq* website has an excellent list of commercial photo agencies at: https://www.creativebloq.com/photography/photo-libraries-12121413.

- The National Library of Australia entry point for finding and purchasing images from their collections: https://www.nla.gov.au/collections/what-we-collect/pictures/using-pictures-collection#findingpic.

- The State Library of Victoria has a selection of royalty-free images here: https://www.slv.vic.gov.au/images.

- As an example of what you can expect to pay, the State Library of NSW has a list of charges (from $22 to $90) for using digital images from their collections at: https://www.sl.nsw.gov.au/research-and-collections/using-library/ordering-digital-images-and-archival-prints.

- There are a number of photographic release form templates available on the Internet, including versions for models and pet animals. Some of these can be customised to your own requirements but you may have to pay a fee or subscribe to a mailing list. Alternatively, searching for 'Photographic release forms Australia' in *Google Images* will give you a good idea of what is required.

- This magazine article discusses the legalities of taking photographs in different locations: http://www.capturemag.com.au/advice/know-you-rights-shooting-in-public.

- Information regarding taking and using photographs of Uluru: https://parksaustralia.gov.au/uluru/do/photography/.

CHAPTER 8

Design

THE DESIGN OF A BOOK, whether the cover or the inside pages, must always work for the benefit of the *reader.* All too often books are produced with a layout that may look pretty but is, in reality, distracting or makes the content difficult to comprehend.

Of course, if you're setting out to produce a beautiful book as a tangible object in its own right — then go for it. Ignore everything that follows and just trust your creative genius. (Note that this chapter does not deal with the practical aspects of typesetting and physically formatting pages because that's covered in Chapter 13 along with information about e-book formatting.)

I'm assuming that by this stage you have decided on the most appropriate size and format for your book (Chapter 1) and checked that it is a standard and economical printing size so you won't be caught out with unexpected extra costs or lots of wasted paper offcuts. It is also worth noting that odd-shaped or large books frequently get bumped to lower, less noticeable shelves in most bookshops.

Cover design

A book cover has several important functions. It is the primary advertisement for your book and it will appear in a number of different locations, not only on bookshop shelves. It must both inform and evoke an emotional response.

It will be reproduced in different sizes, from tiny thumbnails on an online shop web page to big posters at the launch or in a shop window. It needs to accommodate all such formats.

Which one has the most impact?

In a bricks-and-mortar location a cover must have a positive impact on a potential purchaser from, say, the other side of a bookshop. This, in turn, means the design should not be too 'busy' and the customer should immediately gain an idea of the content and tone of the book. You have just a second or two to grab their attention before they tune out and their eyes move on to the next book. Additionally, the fact that a cover may be reproduced digitally in lower quality and at a much smaller size (**thumbnails**) should be taken into account. I would, therefore, urge you to choose a reasonably large type for the title with perhaps a single background image that does not overwhelm the wording.

There has been criticism that this approach has led publishers to create similar 'bold and blocky' cover designs *en masse* for the social media era but the fact is that if you want to sell your book in significant numbers you must give it the best chance of reaching potential customers.

Further, using special effects like glossy spot varnish on matte lamination or metallic foil or raised embossing is fine if it actually draws attention to your book or benefits it in some way. Unfortunately, I've seen many books with expensive design features that are so subtle you don't notice them until after you've picked it up. This might be fine if you're selling the book as a tactile work-of-art but the additional cost may not have any worthwhile marketing benefit. And I'm not convinced these kind of special effects matter at all when so many books are sold online anyway.

Try not to use overly fancy display fonts for the cover unless you're intentionally going for a tactile work-of-art. The more straightforward, the better. And watch out for fonts that produce awkward spacing between certain letters. For example, a capital 'T' next to a 'A' where there is inadequate compensation for the overhang will create an awkard space and sometimes, unintentionally, appear to form two

> "In a badly designed book, the letters mill and stand like starving horses in a field. In a book designed by rote, they sit like stale bread and mutton on the page. In a well-made book ... the letters are alive. They dance in their seats "
>
> Robert Bringhurst, typographer

separate words. This might be fine in a small size in the body of the text, but in large type on the cover it will look terrible.

A subtitle should be short yet descriptive. Avoid over-explaining the contents with long subtitles or superfluous superlatives. You could add an extra teaser line — but don't overdo it. If the cover is cluttered it could be symptomatic of the text. If you get someone interested enough, they will pick it up to learn more. There's more about titles and subtitles in Chapter 1.

And let's not forget the back cover. All kinds of stuff gets dumped here, but it really needs only the blurb, a note about the author, plus the bar code and perhaps a short list of the relevant genres or categories. Again, it's best to keep it neat and tidy, not full of unnecessary text or quotes. See Chapter 16 for more about blurbs — and keeping them short.

Text design

There's a tendency for writers producing their first book to jump straight into whatever the template for 'books' or 'publication' happens to be on their computer program. *Urgh.* There is nothing worse than seeing pages with one centimetre of space all the way around the edge, with the text crammed up tight, simply because that's the way the template has it. You really, really don't have to do it that way.

You will, hopefully, have decided at the outset what your book should look like (Chapter 1). This means there is already a starting point for your design. It might be straightforward text or a magazine-style layout, in black and white or full colour, but whatever you have chosen, there are still some conventions and book design guidelines you need to follow if you want your book to look as professional as possible.

A bit of history

The earliest book designs were based on the handwritten pages drawn by monks in scriptoriums. They would leave space in the outer margins for colourful patterns, embellished lettering, and illustrations. There would be lots of empty space and the text itself would take up approximately half of each page.

These layout principles were (arguably) carried over into the way early European printers laid out the first pages using movable type. If you look at, say, Gutenberg's Bible (*c.* 1455) you will note the same basic idea of wide margins on the outer edges and smaller margins on the inner edge towards the spine. For several hundred years basic page design remained broadly similar, although the size of the spacious margins reduced over time.

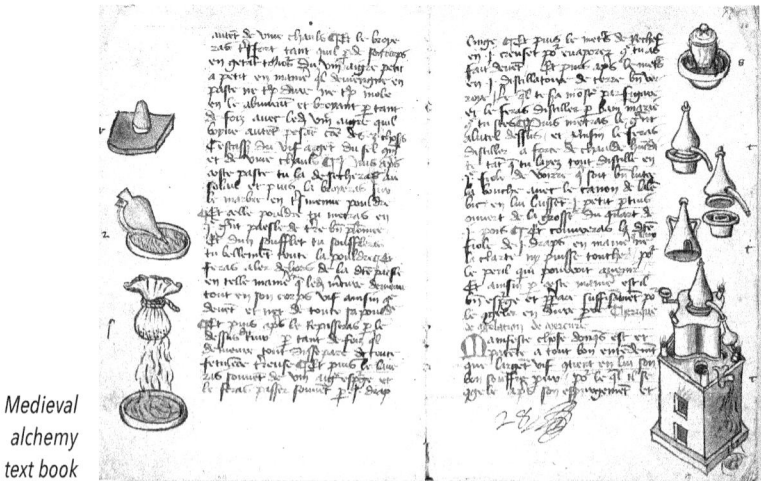

Medieval alchemy text book

There are, of course, always exceptions, but things didn't change greatly until the 20th century when paperbacks began to be mass produced and made more available to the public. Text was pushed further towards now equally-spaced margins, but the new cheaper 'perfect' binding method (pages glued not sewn together) also meant books could not be opened flat without cracking the spine.

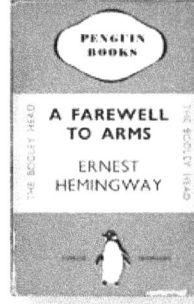

Cheap, mass produced books pioneered by Penguin in 1935

Design principles

Whether or not you are following the advice about finding an existing page format that is suitable for your own book, there are some important considerations for your design:

Adequate margins Wide enough to accommodate the running head (book and chapter titles, and page numbers), and to avoid readers damaging the book by folding the book backwards because lines of type disappear into the spine. In an aesthetic sense, decently sized margins with plenty of white space will also help pages to visually 'breathe' and not appear dense and cramped and off-putting.

Suitable fonts Ones that reinforce the 'feel' of the book, are legible, the right size for comfortable reading, and use no more than a couple of font 'families.' There should be adequate space between each line (still known as 'leading' after the thin strips of lead used in the days of movable metal type) to assist readability.

Illustrations The design must be able to accommodate placement of illustrations and photographic matter, and captions if necessary, in a consistent manner. Will it have full or half-page photographs? Should the margins be extra wide to include small illustrations? If so, do you have enough of these for the whole book?

Knowledge of all fonts

Conventional wisdom has it that **serif** fonts are more suitable than **sans serif** fonts for large and continuous blocks of type and especially book-length work. Research, albeit from more than 20 years ago, shows that serif fonts are easier on the eye and readers are less likely to tire when reading for lengthy periods. **Sans serif** fonts, on the other hand, set up a 'vibration' that may irritate readers after a few paragraphs. Smaller areas of text, such you might see in a magazine-style or heavily-illustrated book with smaller blocks of type, do not seem to have this problem.

Why this should be so is open to debate. Some experts say human eyes have simply become accustomed to serif fonts and over time we will get used to lengthy blocks of san serifs in much the same way. The jury, as they say, is still out. Personally, I have mixed feelings. I can see how some sans serif faces might cause problems, particularly narrow or condensed versions, but there are others, especially those midway between serifs and san serifs, such as *Optima*, that I would have no problem in using for large or ongoing blocks of text.

Serif fonts suitable for text pages include:

Baskerville

Cambria

Caslon

Garamond

Jenson

Minion

Palatino

Sabon

GgTt

Serifs have small, decorative strokes or flourishes usually at the ends of letters

San serif (or semi-sans serif) fonts recommended for books include:

Optima

Helvetica

Roboto

Open Sans

GgTt

Sans serifs have no flourishes

In choosing a suitable font, attention should also be given to the *width* of the individual letters. Some font families, such as *Palatino*, have wide, rounded letters and this will inevitably affect the number of words per line and thus the total number of words you can fit on a page. If space is an issue you may need to consider a narrower face such as *Caslon* or *Cambria*.

I have not included the ubiquitous *Times* and its many derivations in this list because, put simply, it is a condensed font designed specifically for use in the narrow columns of printed newspapers (it was originally commissioned for *The Times* of London). It also has relatively short ascenders and descenders so more lines of type can be packed into a column. A whole page of it in continuous book form can appear dense and perhaps a little daunting for the reader.

The fonts you use for the title page and the headings on the first page of each chapter (the **chapter opening**) do not have to adhere to the same principles. The type can be as bold or as fancy as you like — as long as it is legible. You can use display fonts (sometimes only available in capitals anyway) for this purpose and even include some kind of graphic device or motif to add visual impact. In the past, the design of these pages was supposed to reflect the design of the cover. This, however, has become increasingly rare as covers are often prepared months in advance of the rest of the book going into production with their design often driven by the marketing department.

Obtaining fonts

The computer you are using for your project will have a number of typefaces already installed. Certain word processing or graphic design software may also include some extra fonts. *Google* has a large range of free fonts available to download. Generally, there will be versions of popular typefaces such as *Caslon* or *Helvetica* with subtle differences which will work just as well in your book.

Importantly, if you do decide to buy and download more fonts (esp. display faces) from a library or agency you must always read the fine print about restrictions on use — and check that both your page formatting software and your e-book platform accept

*Back in the days of movable metal type (Letterpress), a compositor would select the required letters from two trays: an **upper case** for capitals and a **lower case** for small letters and numbers.*

that particular kind of font. See EXTRA INFO below for more about font libraries.

Professional designers

You might, by now, have decided you don't possess the necessary skill set to undertake the design work by yourself and need to commission a professional freelance designer. The same general comments in Chapter 5 about freelance editors apply here too: a more experienced and therefore more expensive designer might be a safer bet in the long run; you will need to brief the designer comprehensively so that there is no misunderstanding about your requirements; some advance payment might be requested; and what is your Plan B if something goes wrong? See EXTRA INFO for a link to a list of Australian book designers.

Book design books

I am aware that I have merely skimmed the surface of book design in this chapter. My intention has been to provide just enough information to get you going on your project. Unfortunately, it is not a subject about which you can find detailed information easily nowadays. As far as I know, there are no formal college courses currently available anywhere in Australia and recent books about design are inclined to concentrate on corporate 'publication' design which is not quite the same thing.

Older books about book design, now mostly out of print, tend to have been published before the digital age so although aspects of history and design principles are usually included (along with slightly more esoteric topics like the *Canons of Page Construction* and the *Golden Ratio*), advice about drafting a complete layout in pencil before you start does seem rather absurd today.

However, if you do want to explore the subject further, a few appropriate titles are listed below. You may need to search online or in secondhand bookshops to find some of them or you could try to obtain them via your local library.

The Book: A Cover to Cover Exploration of the Most Powerful Object of Our Time, Keith Houston, W W Norton, 2016.

On Book Design, Richard Hendel, Yale University Press, 1998.

The Design of Books, Adrian Wilson, Reinhold Publishing, first published 1967, reissued 1993.

The Elements of Typographic Style: Version 4.0, Robert Bringhurst, Hartley and Marks Publishers, 4th Edition, 2012.

Just My Type, Simon Garfield, Avery Publishing Group, Illustrated edition, 2012.

Type & Layout: Are you Communicating or Just Making Pretty Shapes?, Colin Weildon, revised edition, Worsley Press, 2005.

EXTRA INFO AND LINKS

- These two articles address the issue of designing covers primarily for thumbnail reproduction: https://www.vulture.com/2019/01/dazzling-blocky-book-covers-designed-for-amazon-instagram.html; https://www.theguardian.com/books/2021/apr/18/in-the-instagram-age-you-actually-can-judge-a-book-by-its-cover.

- The software company *Adobe* has an extensive library which includes the highly-regarded *Caslon*. Fonts may be purchased individually, or downloaded free of charge if you have subscribed to certain *Adobe* products, particularly the *InDesign* application.

- Advice on buying fonts: https://www.fontfabric.com/blog/fonts-licensing-the-ins-and-outs-of-legally-using-fonts/.

- Guidance from a couple of professional designers: https://www.creativebloq.com/features/font-types-a-designers-guide; https://www.ingramspark.com/blog/best-fonts-for-books.

- A list of the top font libraries: https://www.digitalartsonline.co.uk/features/typography/the-17-best-font-websites/.

- A list of recommended websites with free fonts: https://www.creativebloq.com/typography/download-free-fonts-resources-912696.

- The Australian Book Designers Association has a list of members here: https://abda.com.au/members/.

WILLIAM MORRIS AND THE KELMSCOTT PRESS

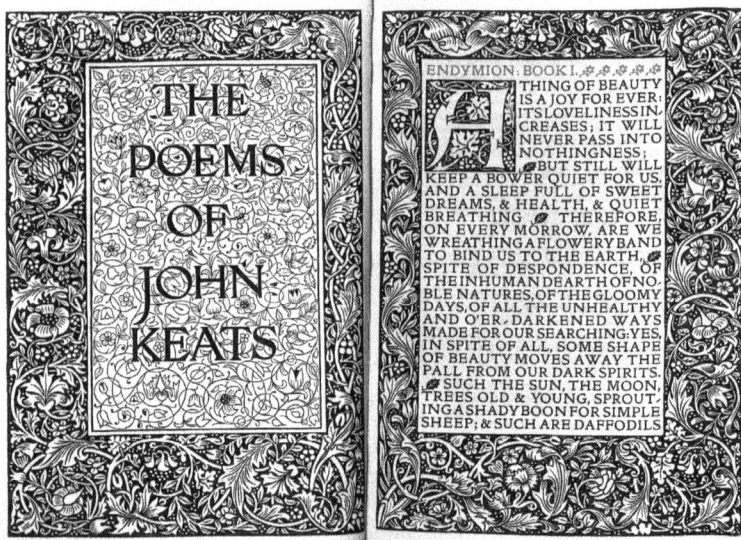

William Morris, the famous social activist and leader of the Victorian era *Arts and Craft* movement, established the Kelmscott Press in London in 1891 with the specific aim of producing books of 'great beauty' with the highest possible standards of quality.

Designs, techniques and materials were all based on those used by printers and craftsmen in the middle ages and extended to replicating 15th century Italian paper made by hand from linen rags. Morris demanded dense black ink which contained few modern chemicals and even designed several new fonts for his books. He believed double-page spreads rather than single pages were the key feature of a book and that opposite pages should complement each other *exactly*. His book on the poems of Keats (shown above) exemplified this approach.

CHAPTER 9

Take a number

EVERY BOOK TITLE must have its own **International Standard Book Number** (ISBN). You can't do much without one. They are used for all kinds of selling, marketing, bibliographic and online data purposes and are the key identifier of a title (and different versions of a title) throughout the world. Moreover, it is very unlikely that retail outlets will stock your book unless it has one.

ISBNs

ISBNs began life in the late 1960s when W H Smith Ltd, the largest book retailer in Britain at the time, set up a new stock control system in their main warehouse and wanted to number-code all the books they held. Several major British publishers came on board and eventually the British Standard Book Number system was introduced. Within a few years the system had been adopted internationally and agencies were set up to allocate the numbers in other countries.

ISBNs had 10 digits originally but by 2007 they were running out of numbers and so introduced 13 digit numbers. You will notice some books, particularly recent reprintings of older books, still show the old 10 digit number as well as the newer 13 digit version on the imprint page.

There are five parts or groups in a 13 digit ISBN. The first set of digits or **prefix element** (978 in the image below) has been supplied by the International Organization for Standardization (ISO) and effectively turns the whole ISBN into an internationally recognised code. The second set (0) is the **registration group** and refers to the language or country of origin. The next set (6487055) or **registrant element** is the publisher's unique identifying number, and the following set (0) refers to the **product** item itself, (or registrant's publication). The final number (5) is a **check digit** arrived at by a mathematical calculation of the previous numbers and enables anyone to confirm that the whole number is valid.

ISBN 978-0-6487055-0-5

9 780648 705505 >

In Australia the ISBN agency is in the hands of **Thorpe-Bowker**, a subsidiary of American bibliographic services company Bowker which is itself affiliated with the multinational data firms *ProQuest* and *Cambridge Information Group*.

To get an ISBN for your book you will need to visit the Thorpe-Bowker website (see EXTRA INFO below) and buy either a single ISBN or a block of 10 if you're planning to follow your amazingly successful first book with lots of others. Each format and edition of your book will require its own ISBN, so if you have a printed version and an e-book, you'll need two. All relevant ISBNs should appear on the imprint page.

When you buy ISBNs or register for any bibliographic database (see below) you will do so as a *publisher*, not an author, so you'll have to come up with a name for your publishing 'firm' and decide whether it also needs to be registered as a formal business name with the Australian Superannuation and Investments Commission (**ASIC**). (See also Chapter 2) Currently, the cost of a single ISBN is $44 and a block of ten is $88. You also need to pay a once-only fee of $55 to register as a publisher. It is worth noting that in other countries, such as Canada, ISBNs are free.

Your printed book will also need a bar code. The ones you buy should be formatted according to the international **EAN-13** standard used in the bookselling industry. Note that the number at the bottom of the barcode will not be the same as the ISBN.

When you order your ISBN from Thorpe-Bowker you may wish to buy an EAN barcode as part of a package. Currently, the cost of a package is $89 for one ISBN and a corresponding barcode. Ten ISBNs and three barcodes will set you back between $199 and $219 depending on whether you want a couple of QRPlus codes as well, and up to five barcodes will cost $45 each. See Chapter 13 for guidance on where to place the barcode.

Cataloguing entry

The **National Library of Australia** (NLA) no longer provides a manual **Cataloguing in Publication** (CiP) service in advance of publication. Once upon a time a library officer would decide on the entry based on a description and perhaps viewing some proofs. Nowadays, you lodge details of your book online and the NLA catalogue entry is generated almost immediately.

I recommend you take a quick look at the **Prepublication Data Service** form and gather all the answers before you start. Whether you place the full CiP entry in the actual book (on the imprint page) is up to you, but having an entry at the NLA does mean that libraries around Australia which use their systems or indeed anyone else interrogating their database will find it more easily.

Global Books in Print

This is an important primary database that feeds into a large number of others around the world, including international online sellers like *Amazon* and *Book Depository*. You need to log into the Thorpe-Bowker account which was created when you bought the ISBN block; find your way to *My Account* and then *Edit ISBNs*. Again, complete as much of the information as possible because it will help people find your book easily.

Copyright Agency

While you're busy filling out forms, you should also take at look at pages 71-72 and the process for registering with the Copyright Agency. Registering your book with them will ensure any potential revenue from the statutory licence scheme for photocopying books in educational institutions is sent to the right place.

EXTRA INFO AND LINKS

- Thorpe-Bowker ISBNs: https://www.myidentifiers.com.au/identify-protect-your-book/isbn/buy-isbn;
  Barcodes: https://www.myidentifiers.com.au/barcode/main.

- More information about the ISBN system can be found at: https://www.isbn-international.org.

- Calculating the ISBN check digit: https://isbn-information.com/check-digit-for-the-13-digit-isbn.html.

- National Library of Australia (Canberra): prepublication data service: https://www.nla.gov.au/content/prepublication-data-service.

"If you write what you yourself sincerely think and feel and are interested in, you will interest other people."

Rachel Carsen, writer

CHAPTER 10

Copyright & permissions

SO, IT'S ALL YOURS. Or is it? Some of it might be theirs. If it is, you must get their permission.

At a basic level, **copyright** exists in a work the instant it is created (but not by AI — see EXTRA INFO). The creator owns the copyright and may sell or licence the right to reproduce their work in part or total for a specified amount of time. But — and it's a big *but* — a creator's ownership only lasts for a certain period. It is dictated by government legislation and can vary according whatever is being copyrighted and wherever it is first published.

In written work in Australia, for example, the author owns copyright during her or his lifetime and then their estate owns copyright for 70 years after their death.

In some respects, copyright is *intangible*. In other words, it exists in the *intellectual* content of the work, rather than the physical vehicle on which that content is carried. So, while someone may have purchased a painting on a canvas, the original artist will still own the *reproduction* rights. The same goes for a photograph. Someone might own a photo, perhaps enlarged to poster size, but that still doesn't give them the right to reproduce it elsewhere unless they have permission.

Likewise, in a book, the author will always own the intellectual content, but the publisher owns the physical typesetting or 'surface' of the book. If someone wanted to, say, publish a facsimile of a book, there would be two lots of rights to be negotiated — the intellectual property of the author and the physical 'surface' produced by the publisher. For an e-book this might also be the formatted data file produced by the publisher.

The owner of the copyright in a book is normally indicated on the imprint page together with ©, the internationally recognised symbol for copyright (but see note in EXTRA INFO).

When is permission required?

Most importantly, if you are going to reproduce something in your book that has been created by someone else, you need to get permission from the current owner, and possibly pay them a fee for the right to do so.

There are, nevertheless, certain circumstances in which you do *not* need permission to reproduce someone else's work. If it is in the **public domain**, for example, or covered by **Creative Commons** arrangements, or falls under **fair use** provisions, you may be able to reproduce the work without permission as long as you give full and appropriate credit.

In general, something is said to be in the public domain when it has fallen out of copyright. This usually happens once the work is either more than a certain number of years old or the author has been dead for the appropriate number of years.

There are a few other quirks. For instance, all text created and published in the United States before 1923 is automatically in the public domain. Hence, it is always a good idea to check circumstances in the country in which the work originated because, even though copyright is supposed to be a global concept, the actual specifics vary considerably.

As a further example, there was a glitch in Australia in the 1990s when copyright legislation here was slow to catch up with the rest of the world. Lifetime limits were being revised internationally but things got a little out of sync. As a consequence, the work of some notable authors, including George Orwell, accidentally slipped out of copyright in Australia while remaining in copyright nearly everywhere else. So, check.

Creative Commons covers material not in the public domain but for which the creator has waived some rights. Users may reproduce work without formal permission as long as they give appropriate attribution. There are various forms of licensing so it is always best to check the available *Fact Sheets* from Creative Commons Australia to see which one applies.

The **fair use** provision also allows for a relatively small amount of copyrighted material to be reproduced under certain circumstances. It is mostly a legal defence when material is used for purposes of review or academic discussion, particularly in educational or non-profit publications. Again, the definition of fair use varies between countries so you should download one of the relevant Copyright Council *Fact Sheets* mentioned below if you are planning to go down this path.

Copyright advice

The **Australian Copyright Council** is the officially recognised peak body for all matters involving copyright. They publish regularly updated *Fact Sheets* about every conceivable aspect of copyright and you should equip yourself with some of these sheets as soon as you start work on your book. (See EXTRA INFO)

Don't put this off and try to get away with copying something created by someone else. It is very likely they *will* notice. Indeed, some corporate copyright holders are proactive and aggressive in trying to identify infringements and pursuing penalties. Some use specially developed software to scan the Internet for text, images, audio and video which might belong to them. Don't risk it — always check.

Copyright Agency

This similar-sounding organisation is responsible for operating the national **statutory copyright licensing scheme**. Under this, schools, universities and other educational institutions pay an annual fee for a licence which allows them to legally photocopy or electronically share parts (up to 10 percent or one chapter, whichever is greater) of books and other copyrighted documents for their students.

In theory, each time an institution photocopies a page from your book, a small fee will eventually flow on to you. However, it is not literally *every* time — the Agency undertakes an annual sampling of work being photocopied or shared electronically by a range of institutions around the country and extrapolates the results across the titles registered with them. It is interesting to note that some academic textbooks which frequently have big chunks reproduced by universities can potentially make more money this way than through sales of the actual book.

To begin the registration process you need to contact the Agency by email. You can do this at any time, it doesn't have to be before your book is published, but make sure you do it soon after so you don't miss an annual sampling cycle. (See EXTRA INFO*)*

There is another similar system for a form of royalties to flow to authors when their book is borrowed from a public or institutional library. The federal government Lending Rights scheme is in two parts — **Public Lending Rights (PLR)** and **Educational Lending Rights (ELR)** — and requires you to register by 31 March each year for books published in the previous 12 months. Again, EXTRA INFO below has web addresses with contact details.

Getting permission

Once you have determined that you actually *do* need to get permission from someone else, you should attempt to discover the actual owner of the work. Obviously, if the work in question is from a particular website, you should search the site for contact information. Otherwise, a simple *Google* search using the caption may turn up an address or two. A more sophisticated search for the origin of an image can be performed using the *Google* reverse image search function. (See EXTRA INFO)

In any event, you will probably need to get whatever permission you need in writing. The sample form at the end of this chapter shows the information you should provide and also makes it easy for the other party to sign and return. You don't have to use this exact letter format or wording but the information required won't vary significantly. It is increasingly common for this kind of thing to be done by email with the form printed out, signed, scanned and emailed back to you by the other party.

Getting permission can take time. It is unlikely small organisations will have a person on this task full-time and it will be a low priority for them, so if you have tight deadlines you may need to find out who the relevant person is for follow up purposes.

If you are using an image from a photo library — probably applying and paying online — make sure you read the small print so you know the precise conditions of the licence and the circumstances in which you are allowed to use the image. There may be limitations on using it for certain commercial purposes.

It is also worth reading the section in the Copyright Council *Fact Sheet* on photography about getting permission from people whose image or likeness appears in photos. In some circumstances you may need get the subject's permission in writing using a formal **release form** (See also Chapter 7).

Giving permission

Other bodies — commercial publishers or educational institutions, for example — may seek permission *from* you to reproduce parts of your book in one of their own publications. It's up to you whether you give permission freely or charge a fee. If they don't send you a proforma return letter like the one shown at the end of this chapter, you can create your own based on the examples shown.

You may even be approached by someone wanting to use the content for other purposes, such as in a movie or a television show. Even dour works of non-fiction can end up being used dramatically. Professor Manning Clark's six-volume *A History of Australia* was turned into a (albeit short-lived) stage musical, so don't think it can't happen. There's some more about licensing your various intellectual rights in Chapter 20.

Acknowledgments and credits

You must always acknowledge the copyright of an item you are using that is not yours. Indeed, if you obtain formal permission to use something, the copyright holder may stipulate the precise form of words you should use. Depending on the design of your book you could add the credit to the caption or create a special page for all acknowledgments at the end of the book.

Plagiarism

Taking the work of others and passing it off as your own is not just unfair and deceptive, it is a form of theft. So, don't. You might think you can rip off a few lines from *Wikipedia* or elsewhere online without attribution and pretend you've written it, but there is a high chance someone, somewhere will be suspicious. All they need to do is run the text through one of the many plagiarism checking programs available and you'll be found out.

EXTRA INFO AND LINKS

- The primary international treaty on copyright is the Berne Convention of 1886 and numerous revisions since. It is overseen by the World Intellectual Property Organisation, an agency of the United Nations. Only a handful of countries have failed to sign up to the Convention.

- The global copyright symbol © reinforces ownership of the work but under the Berne Convention its use is not mandatory.

- In some countries (especially in Europe) authors like to add a line asserting their *moral rights* as a further form of protection against their work being tampered with, even if it has been assigned to a third party. It is not necessary in Australia: https://www.artslaw.com.au/information-sheet/moral-rights/.

- Copyright Agency information and membership: https://www.copyright.com.au/ membership/join-us/. (memberservices@copyright.com.au).

- The Australian Copyright Council has an extensive website with a collection of downloadable information sheets here: https://www.copyright.org.au/resources.

- Information about lending rights: https://www.arts.gov.au/funding-and-support/lending-rights-schemes-elrplr.

- How to do a *Google* reverse image search: https://support.google.com/websearch/answer/1325808?

- Information about Creative Commons is available here: https://au.creativecommons.net/using-cc-material/.

- Plagiarism checker: https://www.grammarly.com/plagiarism-checker.

- Text produced by artificial intelligence (AI) cannot be copyrighted. Additionally, AI software may 'scrape' already copyrighted information and thus infringe existing intellectual property ownership.

SAMPLE PERMISSION REQUEST

[Name]

[Full postal address]

[Telephone number optional]

[Date]

Dear _____ [Name]

I am currently writing a guide for commercial publication about choosing and raising your own pet unicorn. The book is entitled *The Unicorn's New Family* and is scheduled to be published in Australia in January 2024 as a paperback with a print print run of 2,000 copies, and also as an e-book. The retail price will be $32.95 for the printed book and $19.95 for the e-book.

I am writing to request permission to include in this book the material shown on the attached photocopy. Full acknowledgment and credit will be given to the source. If you are prepared to grant permission, please sign and return the attached form of approval and/or advise me of any fee payable.

If you do not hold the copyright to this work, I would be grateful if you would forward this letter to the appropriate person or entity, or advise me accordingly.

Yours sincerely,

[Signed]
[Full name]

SAMPLE PERMISSION GRANTING

To: _____ *[Name]*

Approval is hereby granted for the following material to be reproduced in a book entitled *[Title]* being *[self-]* published in Australia by *[Name]*.

Brief description and source *[book title and page number]* of material for which permission is requested:

_____

_____

_____

Acknowledgment of this material must be given in the following form:

_____

_____

_____

I confirm that I or the organisation I represent hold the copyright to this material and that I am authorised to give this permission.

Signed: _____

Date: _____

Full name and designation if applicable: _____

_____

Contact details: _____

CHAPTER 11

_____

Imprint

THE IMPRINT PAGE contains all the 'small print' for the book and is normally printed on the reverse of the title page. Booksellers and librarians will look here for basic bibliographic data and other information so it must be accurate and complete. If the information is not placed here in its usual spot, it will appear — often in even smaller type — on the last printed page of the book.

The first part, at the top of the page, features the name and contact details of the publisher, and the logo if you've got one.

[Logo]

Book Publisher Name
PO Box 500, Whereville
Stateland 9876, Australia

www.publisherimprint.org
enquiries@publisherimprint.com.au

You may choose to include a postal address or an email address or both or just let people find their way via the *Contact us* section on your website (see Chapter 16 on Marketing).

This is followed by the publication date and edition, if appropriate, and details of the copyright owners or licence holders.

First published 2022
Fifth edition, 2024
Text © Author Name 2024
Design and typography © Book Publisher Name 2024

As noted previously, copyright of the design and typography (or 'surface') belongs to the publisher, not the author.

Although not obligatory, publishers sometimes include the names of people involved in producing the book who may not be acknowledged elsewhere. For example:

Publisher: Jasmine Greaves
Production coordinator: Rob Moore
Copyeditor: Norma Styles
Designer: Jeff Hirst
Typesetter: Rae Wilson
Printed by Stadium Print

Then come the ISBNs. The full list should include numbers for all versions and editions currently available: paperback, hardback, e-book (EPUB), and e-book (PDF) if you have one.

ISBN XXXXXXXXXXXX (paper)
ISBN XXXXXXXXXXXX (EPUB)
ISBN XXXXXXXXXXXX [PDF]

A statement about copyright appears next and reference is usually made to the statutory licence scheme (See Chapters 9 and 10). Some publishers omit this line because they would prefer people remain in the dark about the scheme and buy the actual book rather than photocopy bits of it.

There are various kinds of disclaimers you could include. The one here relates to websites mentioned, and other possible legal ramifications. You would also be wise to disclaim liability for certain kinds of advice you provide in your book, especially if it concerns food, health or wellbeing.

Then there's the **Prepublication Data Service** entry from the **National Library of Australia**. Once you have entered bibliographic details of your book, the full entry pops up as if by magic on their database. You can copy it but it is not mandatory and (especially if you're short of space) you could just add the line 'A catalogue entry for this book is available from the National Library of Australia.' The Library provides a small graphic file publishers may download from the NLA website which incorporates their logo and preferred wording.

A catalogue record for this book is available from the National Library of Australia

Finally, you should formally thank any organisation which has contributed to production of the book financially or by providing services in kind.

The author and publisher acknowledge with thanks the assistance of the Queensland Foundation for the Promotion of Unicorns in financially supporting publication of this book.

Acknowledgments and credits for illustrations and photographs do not normally appear on the imprint page; they go either next to the image itself or in a list on another page, usually at the very end of the book. The only exception would be to credit a cover image.

EXTRA INFO AND LINKS

National Library of Australia, Canberra: catalogue entry, statement and logo: https://www.nla.gov.au/cataloguing-statement.

CHAPTER 12

E-book publishing

INCREASINGLY, book buyers expect that titles will be available in both print and electronic formats and also sometimes as an audiobook. Millions of **e-books** are available to instantly download and start reading and they are considerably cheaper than their print counterparts

Yet it appears that after years of growth — and despite a general perception that e-books would one day replace printed books entirely — the novelty appears to be wearing off. In recent years sales of e-books (and their reading devices) have plateaued and in some cases gone into noticeable decline, whereas sales of printed books have increased significantly (in certain genres by slightly more than 12 percent) and continue to grow.

Publishing an e-book is certainly a cost-effective, and to some extent hassle-free, way to get your work in front of a audience. It may even get you noticed by a mainstream publisher. It can certainly be much more profitable than print, given that the author usually does most of the work at no cost and there are no major distribution expenses. In other words, you get to keep most of the cash.

The two main sales outlets for e-book publishing are **iBooks** (*Apple*) and **Kindle** (*Amazon*). While there are a few others, such as **Kobo**, they do not currently appear to have the same extensive market reach. If you have issues with using these massive multinationals and want to explore releasing via Australia-owned booksellers, be aware they might simply be a shopfront for a multinational. The Australia online retailer Booktopia, for example, currently partners with Kobo.

You could use an e-book distribution agency such as **Smashwords** to feed your book to all available e-book retailing platforms but they will (inevitably) take a cut and reduce the final amount going into your bank account. Another option might be to deal directly with the biggest two outlets (Apple and Amazon) and delegate distribution to others through an agency.

Alternatively, you could sell a PDF version directly through your own website. This relies heavily on marketing the book yourself and somehow ensuring everyone who might buy it actually gets to hear about it.

In theory you can choose your own retail price point but sellers will 'encourage' you to keep prices under a certain level (say, at $9.99 or $12.99) by offering different royalty structures. So, pay careful attention to the small print when you upload to these larger sellers because there can be a wide disparity in

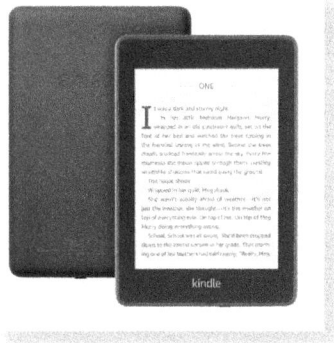

potential royalties (30 percent to 70 percent of the retail price) depending on the terms and conditions.

Finally, it should be noted that the retail pricing of e-books has become a contentious issue in recent years. There is pressure to reduce retail price levels for consumers (reflecting the lower cost of production), while at the same time many authors would prefer higher prices and thus better royalties.

The actual, technical task of formatting your book for e-book publication is covered in the next chapter.

EXTRA INFO AND LINKS

- Further information about e-book publishing key players :

  Amazon: (Kindle) https://kdp.amazon.com/en_US/; also, see details of their pricing structure here: https://kdp.amazon.com/en_US/help/topic/G200634560.
  Apple: (iBooks) https://support.apple.com/en-au/HT201183.
  Kobo: (an anagram of 'book') is based in Canada but owned by a Japanese conglomerate: https://www.kobo.com/au/en/p/writinglife.

- Details of the Smashwords e-book distribution agency is here: https://www.smashwords.com/about/how_to_publish_on_smashwords.

- LightningSource (Ingram) is mentioned in Chapter 15 and again on page 162 in the context of printing services but it also acts as an e-book distribution agency and will ensure your e-book is available through major providers and listed on *Amazon* and other online retailers: https://www.ingramspark.com/features.

CHAPTER 13

Typesetting & formatting

BY NOW YOU SHOULD have finished writing and collecting all the images for your book and you should have the design concept nicely tucked away in your head. Even better, you have in your possession a copy of the book on which your design will be based. Time to get the thing down in a form to send to a printer or an e-book file to upload and publish.

Whether you're intending to publish in one or the other or both formats, the starting point for typesetting is the same: you must use the **styles** function in your word processing program. By applying a specific style to headings, paragraphs, lists and so on, formatting will be consistent throughout the book and it will convert more easily to a page layout or e-book format.

It is therefore vital that you familiarise yourself with the way styles work for headings and textual matter in whichever word processing software you use — more than likely Microsoft **Word**™ or Apple **Pages**.™ If you don't already know how to apply them, you might find it helpful to follow one of the tutorials built into the relevant software or perhaps find your way to a **YouTube**™ instructional video. (See EXTRA INFO)

Your first task is make absolutely sure your manuscript is complete and final in all senses of both of those words. You must also have everything else you need in the way of illustrations and photographs, scanned at the correct **dpi** (see Chapter 7) and tidied away in unambiguously named folders on your computer. There are now two different pathways:

- a PDF document formatted to your printer's specifications.

- a file suitably formatted for turning into an e-book.

Typesetting for print

The correct tools

Although it is technically possible to format a book using a word processing program, there are significant limitations in what you can achieve and the end result may not give you the best or most professional-looking level of quality. There is also the issue of being able to export the file to the exact PDF specifications stipulated by your printer.

Of course, if you are planning to produce something quite simple in, say, A4 and spiral-bound at a local print shop, then go ahead, there's nothing to stop you using *Word* or *Pages*. Both will allow you to use different fonts, adjust margins and insert running headings with page numbers. You will be able to insert breaks to indicate the beginning of new chapters or sections and place illustrations or photos in the appropriate positions. So don't let me stop you.

However, if you want your book to look, ahem, *professional*, it is important that you use appropriate page layout software. The longtime industry leaders are Quark Inc's **QuarkXPress™** and Adobe's **InDesign™**. At the time of writing, *QuarkXPress* is available with an annual licence for $332.52 (extra if you want automatic updates) and *InDesign* is available with an annual subscription of $343.07, although it can also be paid at $29.99 per month. An ongoing monthly subscription that doesn't lock you in is currently $45.99. There are discounts for customers in educational settings. A more recent and increasingly popular alternative is **Affinity Publisher™** which has a huge price advantage over the others (currently a one-off $64.99 with a 40 percent discount) but it does lack a number of features.

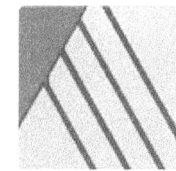

Both *QuarkXPress* and *InDesign* form part of suites of compatible software produced by both companies. Both include photo-editing and PDF management applications. *InDesign* is part of Adobe's **Creative Cloud™** suite which costs $79.99 per month for all of their standard applications including **Photoshop™** and **Acrobat™**. Before buying any of these items of software, you must make sure your computer system is technically compatible and has enough processing power to accommodate the very large applications — and always check current prices and discounts.

As with word processing, it would also be useful if you could watch **YouTube** videos that relate to your specific layout program if you intend to use one — at least the basic or introductory concepts — so you don't have to constantly stop and start when you're working on the formatting. Be aware, however, that some *YouTube* tutorials, informative though they may be, are sometimes used as bait to entice you into longer and more comprehensive online courses that charge a juicy fee. (See EXTRA INFO)

Dos and don'ts

Finding your way around a sophisticated typesetting and page layout program for the first time can be daunting. Hopefully, by viewing *YouTube* and using the program's own embedded manual you will master it in no time. Even so, there are a number of issues over which newbies invariable stumble. I'll run through them briefly:

Fonts   Mostly covered in Chapter 8 but you must ensure that the category of font you have chosen is technically compatible with your software. For example, **OpenType** fonts are currently an industry standard, whereas older **TrueType** fonts *may* have some technical issues. The whole font family (italics, bold, condensed, extra bold etc) should be acquired and downloaded to your computer's font folder. Try not to get confused by the way font sizes (and other layout measurements) are sometimes described in points and sometimes in millimetres.

Spacing   *Leading* refers to the space between individual lines of type. In general, the amount of space applied here can affect the readability of the text. It would be wise to road test different amounts of space to determine the most suitable amount.

Kerning refers to the space between individual characters and although default kerning is usually fine, it may need a little tweaking to aid readability. This is especially true if you are using a condensed font.

Paragraphs The decision whether to leave a clear line space between paragraphs or to follow on and indent the beginning of the next paragraph will, obviously, depend on the design you have chosen. In a 'traditional' book I would expect to see an indent and no extra space between lines in the body of the text. The amount you indent should depend on your design rather than the default set by the program you are using. However, if you *are* leaving a space, note that it should not be a full blank line but a function of the 'space after paragraph' function and would normally be set at just a few extra points.

Hyphenation Page layout programs will allow you to automatically hyphenate the text. It is most useful when there are paragraphs where some lines are jam-packed with text and other lines with big gaps between words. In theory, hyphenation will break words between syllables and allow the text to even out. However, it can also result in some unhappy situations with breaks occurring at the end of multiple consecutive lines or perhaps breaks at awkward points or in unfortunate places and not necessarily between syllables. This seems to happen most often if the dictionary embedded in your software is set to American spelling rather than Australian or British. In such cases it may be better to turn off hyphenation for that paragraph and use 'soft returns' and manually inserted hyphens instead.

world in the 1990s have increas-
·balisation'. The term has econ-
aspects. In the economic sense
·ess whereby markets, economic
ted on a global scale. In its tech-
the rapid advances in commun-
1at have facilitated greater inter-
The concept has been interpreted
1at have gradually overwhelmed

O f all the great rivers of the world, none is as intriguing as
the Pearl. Short by world standards, it epitomizes the
old expression that good things come in small pack-
ages. Though the Pearl measures less than 50 miles in total
length from its modest source as a cool mountain spring to the
screaming cascades and steaming estuary of its downstream
reaches, over those miles, the river has in one place or another
everything you could possibly ask for. You can roam among
lush temperate rain forests, turgid white water canyons, con-
templative meanders among aisles of staid aspens (with trout
leaping to slurp all the afternoon insects from its calm surface), and forbidding swamp land as formidable as any that
Humphrey Bogart muddled through in *The African Queen*.

Typesetting problems. Too many consecutive line breaks (left) and a distracting white 'river' in the middle of a paragraph (right). Fixed by adjusting word breaks or by tweaking the kerning.

Headings   Headings are headings, not just another line of text. They should stand out on their own by being noticeably larger than the body text or perhaps in bold or italic or capitals instead. They do not need to be underlined or have colons (:) placed at the end. If you have more than one level of heading, make sure the hierarchy is clear, and don't let subheadings be mistaken for an ordinary line of text. Running headings at the top (or running feet at the bottom) contain the book title (left side of page or *verso*) and chapter title (right-hand page or *recto*) and should be above the body text, positioned so that they cannot be mistaken for the text itself. They are often set in a smaller size and different font for this reason.

Widows and orphans   These are traditional terms for a single line of text from the beginning or end of a paragraph which finds itself all alone at the bottom (orphan) or top (widow) of a page. In conventional typesetting practice, such aberrations are usually dealt with by reducing or increasing the number of lines on a page and thus pushing the dangling line forwards or pulling it back. Unfortunately this is not as simple as it sounds because, strictly speaking, text blocks on facing pages need to align so you would also have to change lines on the opposite page. This might introduce other problems. It is therefore becoming increasingly common to leave a widow or an orphan alone unless it looks awkward, such when there is a single word at the top of a page.

Double spaces   It is almost certain that when you learned to type you were taught to leave two spaces between each sentence. There are lots of theories about why this should have been insisted upon (see EXTRA INFO) but there is no logical reason for it, and although the practice is slowing dying out many typesetters still find they have to spend time removing all the superfluous spaces before they can begin. If this has happened in your manuscript, the extra spaces can be removed by performing a 'search-and-replace' while it is still at the word processing stage but care must be taken to check every 'hit' in case there is a genuine reason for two spaces to exist at that point. Thankfully, later versions of Microsoft *Word* flag two spaces as an error.

Dashes and quote marks   Turn on 'curly' or 'typesetters' quote marks (" "). See the separate box about dashes on page 101.

Cover

The cover needs to be formatted as a complete item: front, back and spine all on the same layout spread. Until this point you will probably have been working on single text pages and won't have been concerned about things like bleed or blocks of colour.

To arrive at the total dimensions of the layout you will need to obtain the spine width. Unless you're prepared to make a huge guess and perhaps adjust things later, you cannot do this until you have finished formatting the text pages and know the total page extent.

Most printers will calculate the spine width for you once you confirm the total extent and have chosen the paper stock for your book. (See Chapter 14 for more about paper and card)

Printers are very touchy about the way covers are formatted. Indeed, once you have a final page extent, some printers may provide a pre-formatted layout file with the correct dimensions in order to reduce potential errors. **LightningSource**, for example, will supply a cover template for you to use before exporting the file to their PDF specifications.

There are several key differences in formatting a cover as opposed to text pages:

Bleed   It is inevitable that you will have images or blocks of colour extending to the very edge of the cover. Importantly, these need to physically extend *past* the actual edge to allow for slight inaccuracies when the book is trimmed to size. This is known as the **bleed** with images and so on being *bled-off.* The bleed area should extend at least 3 mm past all edges of the cover. It will be cut off so it must not contain any important details.

Safe zone   This is the area of the cover containing typography or images or blocks of colour ('objects') which are safe from being accidentally cut off when the finished book is trimmed to size. Printers say you should leave 5 mm clear all around the edge for this purpose but this has always seemed excessive to me and, frankly, it would be a massive technical stuff-up for this much to be over-trimmed.

Trim marks   These are short lines extending outside the layout grid which will appear on the printed sheets and indicate where the cover should be trimmed. They do not appear in the finished

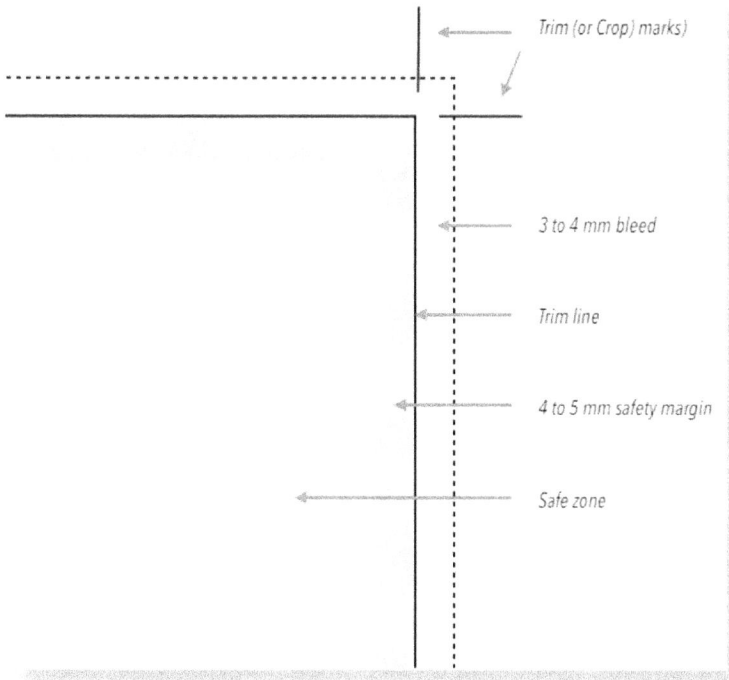

Trims and bleeds

book. Conventional printers specify them but they are not usually required for books printed digitally. You should check with your chosen printer.

Spine The spine contains the name of the author, title of the book, and publisher's logo or name. Wording runs from top to bottom, meaning it faces to the left. Spines that are wide enough sometimes include the subtitle. When you are typesetting the spine it is likely that you will use different type sizes (or even different fonts) for the title and the author name. It is therefore sensible to place the text for these in different text boxes when positioning them because both sets of words should be in the *centre* of the spine (side to side), not along the same base line.

Fold marks
Fold marks

Caring For Your Pet Unicorn   Booky McBook

Bleed   Trim mark   All text inside safe zone   Trim mark   Bleed

Spine lines

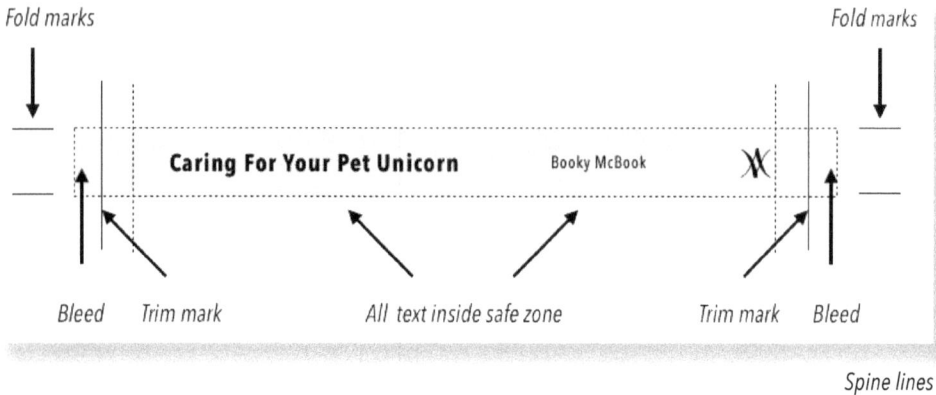

Barcode   In theory, this can appear anywhere on the back cover but booksellers will generally expect it to be positioned on the right-hand side towards the bottom. It must be in the standard EAN format and be machine-readable which usually means black on white reproduction (even though in theory barcodes can be printed in a range of colours) and not too small.

Colour   The cover is the most likely place for you to use blocks of colour, especially for all or part of the background. However, you need to be aware when viewing a particular colour on your computer screen it might not appear *exactly* the same when printed. The colours on your screen are produced from combinations of three primary colours referred to as **RGB** (Red, Green and Blue) whereas the colours produced by conventional printing are produced by a combination of four coloured inks known as **CMYK** (Cyan, Magenta, Yellow and K for black). This could lead to unexpected variations in the printed version, especially if you have pale or subtle colours so it would be sensible to ask for a printed (paper) proof rather than a digital one to be absolutely sure it hasn't changed noticeably.

Final output

Layout programs will allow you to export the file to a range of PDFs with different specifications. Your printer will tell you which one they want. Do not be alarmed if the version they require seems old — it probably has fewer 'bells and whistles' with less potential for technical glitches. There are a couple of other issues to watch out for when you are getting the file ready to export:

Graphics pathway When you place an illustration or any kind of image on the layout the software automatically creates a link to the folder in your computer where it is stored. If for any reason you move the image to an different folder or location the software gets very confused and may not reproduce the image correctly — or perhaps not at all. So, once you have positioned images, leave the originals where they are or you will have to laboriously reestablish the pathway before exporting the file.

Colour Double-check that your printer requires colour items to be in CMYK. (See *colour* in the section above) You may have to convert them as appropriate before exporting.

E-book formatting

Hopefully, you have already read Chapter 12 about the differences between e-book formats and publishing platforms because it may influence the way you format the text for an e-book. A PDF or a *fixed* EPUB is relatively simple to produce, being an exact replica of the print edition, but an e-book in a *flowing* format requires some extra work. You might decide you need both versions to satisfy your potential market.

Again, it is essential you apply *styles* when finalising your text (as per the print version). Once you get the hang of them, they are quick and easy to apply. When the text is converted to a flowing EPUB format using a suitable piece of software, the various elements will be automatically converted to the appropriate style.

The styles function can also be used to insert hyperlinks which will enable users to jump to other parts of the e-book. This is particular useful for the contents page where the links are based on the chapter headings. In addition, users will also expect to click on web addresses and be magically transported to the relevant locations. It is especially important to check that all web links are all still live and have not dropped out in the conversion process.

PDF

There are two possible starting points when creating a PDF e-book:

From a word processing document *(eg. Word or Pages)* Both Apple and Windows operating systems will allow you to convert a word processing document to a PDF file. It will be fairly basic, probably using pre-installed Adobe *Acrobat* software, and you will have little say on the level of quality. Do not use *export* for this purpose: the options are limited. Instead you need to click on *print* in the pull-down menu and the PDF option will appear towards the bottom of the panel. Choose the relevant security or permissions options to place certain conditions on use of the file, such as limiting it to view-only so it cannot be edited or copied. If you want a different level of visible quality or perhaps a wider range of restrictions on how the file can be used — such as reducing the quality significantly when it is printed out — you should import the file into the separate Acrobat *Distiller* software.

From page layout software *(eg. InDesign or Quark)* Once you have completed formatting and saved the file, you can export the whole document or just a selection of pages to PDF. By this stage the document should already be in the correct size. Again, there are a range of options and you should choose the output format most suited to your needs. Avoid output formats configured specifically for high-end printing and take care to exclude elements such as crop marks or colour registration marks or patterns.

Whichever of the above methods you use to transform your document into a PDF, you must add the front cover before you export the file, so it forms part of the whole document.

EPUB – fixed or flowing?

While word processing and page layout programs will allow you to convert pages straight to a *fixed* format in just a few clicks, the many potential glitches that can occur when formatting the *flowing* version may result in many hours of work to put right. You will need to consider whether the extra time, clunky formatting and missing elements are really worth it.

To produce an e-book in a *flowing* format you will need to return to your raw word processing document and convert it from there. Ensure the text corresponds *exactly* with the text on final pages you have formatted for the print edition. If you have made lots of changes the same alterations must be taken into the word processing document.

If this is too difficult for any reason, possibly because there are so many changes, especially fiddly little ones, you might find it easier to convert the formatted pages back into *Word* or *Pages*. However, this will also mean going through it thoroughly to check for poor formatting and to revert things like forced line breaks and stray hyphens. So, swings and roundabouts.

Start with a copy of the final manuscript text file (eg. in *Word* or *Pages*), which hasn't been formatted in any other way apart from having styles applied. This means there should be no headings or page numbers or anything similar. If you have already formatted the text with these elements, strip them out before you do anything else.

There are only a limited range of fonts that work successfully on EPUB e-books and it is therefore wise to use a reasonably plain one for the text — and especially one that has a complete 'family' of bold and italic faces. Avoid fancy display fonts for headings because the software will simply replace them with default typefaces and probably ruin the look you want.

If your book contains illustrations or photographs they must already be in the correct position in the body of the text. Remember that there is usually a single column in a flowing e-book so the illustrations cannot be alongside the text, only between lines or paragraphs. You may need to reposition them in your word processing document first. You also need to ensure the photos are in JPEG and not TIFF and relatively low-res otherwise the software may chuck a wobbly and not load them at all.

A big technical issue when converting a document concerns between-paragraph spacing. Even with the correct settings the conversion process may unexpectedly collapse multiple blank lines into a single line or even try to do away with them altogether, with the text running on endlessly without any kind of break. You may also find that unless you insert a page break *immediately* after the very last full point of a chapter, the software will develop a mind of its own and randomly insert a blank page before the next chapter.

Hence the need to check that the conversion has been successful by viewing the book in its finished form. You may have to do this several times given the amount of adjusting and jiggling involved. You can see how the completed book will look in *Kindle* by downloading the **Kindle Previewer**. (See EXTRA INFO)

Professional typesetters

The principles outlined in Chapters 5 and 8 regarding commissioning freelancers are relevant here as well. A key difference being that professional typesetters will often charge a set amount per page (which may vary depending on the inherent complexity) rather than an hourly rate.

EXTRA INFO AND LINKS

- Advice on applying styles in *Word*: https://www.louiseharnbyproofreader. com/blog/formatting-your-book-in-word-how-to-save-time-with-the-styles-tool.

- More advice about creating an EPUB book from a *Word* document: https://www.janefriedman.com/word-epub/.

- Tutorials on the styles function in *Word*: https://www.youtube.com/watch?v=iUJzijf9rUQ.

- Tutorials for Apple *Pages*: https://support.apple.com/en-au/guide/pages/tanaa39b0aa3/11.0/mac/1.0.

- An interesting discussion about choosing between the two main layout programs (but check current prices): https://appleinsider.com/

articles/19/07/18/how-to-pick-between-indesign-quarkxpress-and-other-publishing-apps.

- Information about *QuarkXPress*: https://www.quark.com/products/quarkxpress.

- Details of the Adobe *Creative Cloud* suite which includes InDesign: https://www.adobe.com/au/creativecloud/plans.html.

- *Affinity Designer* details: https://affinity.serif.com/en-gb/publisher/.

- Online tutorials about using layout programs can run up to a bottom numbing two hours; this basic introduction to *InDesign* goes for 31 minutes: https://www.youtube.com/watch?v=g-lm_rP79C4.

- A comprehensive list of resources for e-book publishing (but I would caution that some of the trade names and links may have changed): https://www.janefriedman.com/how-to-publish-an-ebook/.

- Formatting Apple *Pages* for an e-book: https://www.imore.com/how-create-ebooks-pages.

- A short guide to formatting your book for Amazon *Kindle*: https://kdp.amazon.com/en_US/help/topic/G201723130; and a link to download the *Kindle Viewer*: https://kdp.amazon.com/en_US/help/topic/G202131170.

- Online article discussing the issue of two spaces between sentences: https://slate.com/technology/2011/01/two-spaces-after-a-period-why-you-should-never-ever-do-it.html.

- When not to use hyphens to break a line: https://bhgstylebook.com/breaks/.

- Information about the correct use of *ligatures*, a hang-over from the days of metal typesetting where certain combinations of letters might collide unhappily: https://practicaltypography.com/ligatures.html.

DOING A DASH

Dashes are more commonly known as *rules* and come in three varieties.

A **hyphen** connects two words (usually compound nouns or adjectives) or indicates a break between syllables of a word such as at the end of a line of type. Example: type-face

An **en rule**, so called because it relates to the width of the letter 'n'. It usually appears in spans of numbers, particularly dates and page numbers. It is set without spaces on either side.
Examples: 1956–62; pages 124–136

An **em rule**, based on the width of the letter 'm', is most often used parenthetically and, increasingly, instead of a colon. It can be set with or without spaces but it should be noted that in some fonts em rules can appear quite narrow (eg. in condensed faces such as this one) and be mistaken for a hyphen, drawing separate words together rather than apart as intended.

Examples:

An em without spaces: The unicorns–all of them at this point–were getting nervous about their new neighbours.

An em with spaces: The unicorns – all of them at this point – were getting nervous about their new neighbours.

Interestingly, in some European countries em rules are uncommon and typesetters often use an en rule with spaces on both sides instead.

CHAPTER 14

Paper & card

CHOOSING THE RIGHT paper and cover materials for your book is more important than you might think. They will not only affect its physical appearance but greatly influence a potential customer's perception of value for money. You'll also need to know exactly what materials to ask for when requesting quotes from a printer whether in Australia or overseas.

Everything below should be regarded as general guidance only. There will, inevitably, be variations depending on what is available at the time and the technical preferences of your nominated printer. When in doubt, always get a sample.

I've tried to use **gsm** (grams per square metre) throughout this chapter to describe the weight of paper but some printers, particularly in the USA, like to use *lbs* and *ozs* (pounds and ounces) and these terms have seeped into Australia. Thus, you may need to convert weights using the conversion table mentioned in EXTRA INFO below.

Text paper

Generally, paper used for the text pages in an typical book will be either **coated** or **uncoated**. A coated paper has had a fine layer of china clay or a similar synthetic substance applied to make a smooth, sealed surface. Uncoated papers are, for the most part, everything else.

Gloss, **art**, **satin**, **semi-matte** and **matte** papers are all coated stocks. The principle is the same for all of them — ink sits on the surface of the paper rather than being allowed to soak in or spread. This allows for precise colour registration and enables high quality image reproduction. For this reason, coated paper is nearly always white. Indeed, many books that *appear* to use cream-coated stock are actually white with the non-illustrated areas printed in a light cream colour from edge to edge.

The process of applying the coating on both sides tends to flatten the fibres so, although coated papers might have exactly the same weight as uncoated ones, they are noticeably thinner. This, in turn, means a book with coated paper will be considerably slimmer than one with the same page extent using uncoated paper and this may affect the customer's perception of value for money. Publishers often try to compensate by using heavier gloss paper (from, say, a standard 90 or 100 gsm stock up to 120 gsm or greater) but this can make the book much heavier and is something to consider if large quantities are being sent by ordinary mail.

Uncoated papers, apart from being, you know, uncoated, come in an extraordinary range of weights and thicknesses and shades of white and cream. They are non-reflective and eminently suitable for a wide variety of uses in book production. They can be as thin as tissue for Bibles and large reference books (literally known as **bible paper**), all the way up to almost card-like quality for children's picture books.

Generally, uncoated weight corresponds to thickness — the heavier the paper, the fatter it is, but some lightweight stocks deliberately leave the fibres fluffed up to make the paper *seem* thicker. This 'bulky' paper is frequently used in mass market novels to give the appearance of greater value for money.

Uncoated papers contain mostly wood pulp, some of it recycled (up to 50 percent) and other kinds of filler. The amount of the organic compound **lignin** present in pulp affects the longevity of the paper and contributes to acidity and yellowing. However, it can be treated with chemicals to make it acid-free and less likely to deteriorate over time. In addition, a cocktail of bleach-like chemicals can be added to increase whiteness and improve consistency in appearance across batches.

Many printers will guarantee that the paper they use is manufactured from sustainable sources such as regrowth forests or plantations. The **International Forest Stewardship Council** certifies paper which meets its standards as being partly or fully made from sustainable sources and their tree logo appears on imprint pages as official verification. Other printers say they use only 100 percent recycled paper — even though reprocessed fibres are shorter and liable to detach and produce a great deal of potentially machine-damaging dust.

Weights of text stock can vary between 70 gsm and 120 gsm. A consideration here is the potential for **show-through** which occurs when printed matter on one side of a page is clearly visible on the reverse side. This is less likely to happen with coated stock but it can be problematic with lower weights of uncoated paper. If you are unsure about choosing a paper stock for this reason you should ask your printer for recommendations and obtain samples of pages printed on different weights of paper.

All this is, of course, assuming that your nominated printer will actually *allow* you to choose your own paper. Many do not, primarily because they purchase a small range of paper types in bulk which they then allocate to specific formats of book. Digital printers, in particular, will use only two or three weights of paper for black and white reproduction (eg. 85 gsm or 100 gsm) and will only increase them if the book contains ink-heavy colour pages. Choice of paper stock may also be determined by whether your printer uses a **sheet-fed** machine (eg. single sheets of paper) or a large **web-offset** machine fed by large rolls of paper.

All types of paper and card can be significantly affected by moisture in the atmosphere. A small amount of expansion and contraction of printing sheets due to this is inevitable even when premises are completely sealed and well air-conditioned. When sheets with a higher than normal level of moisture are printed and the resulting folded sections bound into books, they are liable to shrink as they gradually dry, leaving noticeable indentations along the edges of the page block.

Paperback cover

Ideally, card for paperback (sometimes called **limp** or **softback**) covers should be between 240 gsm and 270 gsm. Outside this range the book can become either too floppy or stiff and awkward to open. Again, it is advisable to obtain a sample of the material to be absolutely sure it is what you want.

Bear in mind that whatever weight you choose will probably be covered by some form of **lamination** or **varnish** (see Chapter 15) so the weight and thickness will increase marginally. If cover card is coated at all it is normally only on the outside because the block of text pages is glued directly onto the inside and an uncoated surface provides better adhesion.

Hardback cover

A **hardback** (or **cased**) cover has four main components: the **board** itself, **endpapers** which help to attach the board to the block of pages, the board **covering**, and the **dustjacket**. In the past the board covering would have been linen, thin leather or a textured synthetic material but is it much more common now for it to be a **printed paper covering** which replicates the dustjacket or perhaps eliminates the need for a jacket altogether.

> **Board** Normally formed from grey card, kraft board or mill board. The most suitable weight is around 40 oz (1800 gsm) but can range between 16 oz (1000 gsm) and 48 oz (2200 gsm). Boards may warp if they contain too much moisture when the endpapers are attached and then dry out. Warping may also occur when the grain of the endpaper runs in the

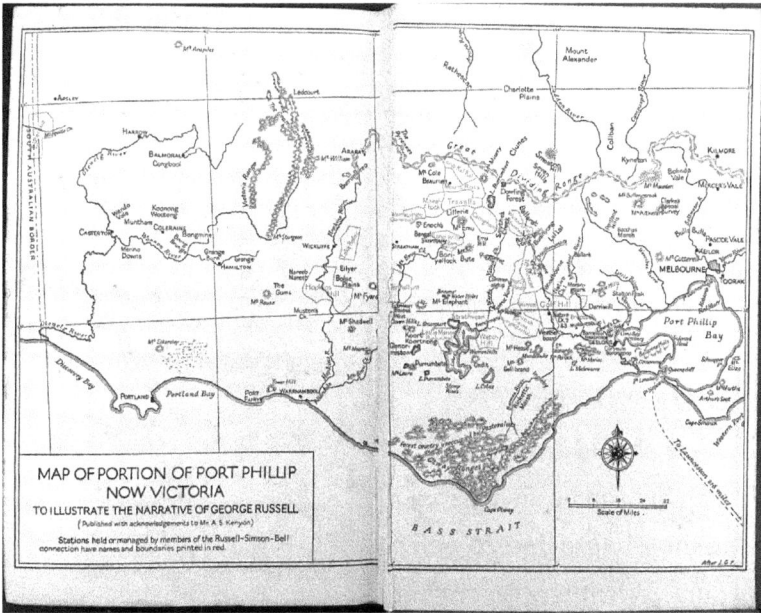

Interesting use of endpapers to display a large map

same direction as the grain in the board instead of being applied at a right angle.

Endpapers These are usually around 110 gsm although the thickness may depend on the book's weight and format size. They help to attach the book block to the board and so the material used has to be sufficiently robust. They can be left plain or printed with an illustration or a patterned design or a block of colour. There was once a craze for unusual types of endpaper, such as marbled patterns or recycled papers embedded with flecks of rag or other unbleached materials but, trust me, your printer will not thank you for specifying these and will probably change extra for the manual work involved in attaching them.

Board covering There are three ways to go with this: a reconstituted or synthetic leather lookalike, a lightly textured **cloth** material, or a fully printed paper covering (or **PPC**). In the past the cloth would have been self-coloured but it is now more likely to be a basic white material printed with whatever colour you desire. Paper for a PPC cover should around 260 gsm but can be anywhere in the 210 gsm to 270 gsm range. A leather-like or cloth cover would normally be

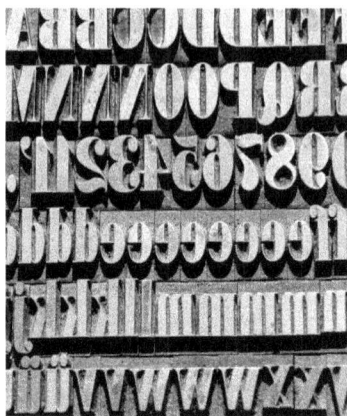

'Brasses' used for embossing book covers

embossed on the spine with at least the title, author name and publisher's logo. (See EXTRA INFO)

Dustjacket Ideally no less than 128gsm. And, as with end-papers, the size and format of the book will affect the weight — the heavier the book, the heavier the dustjacket, so anywhere up to 160 gsm would be acceptable. As with the cover, the dustjacket will probably be laminated so the actual thickness will increase anyway.

Cases can be either round-backed or square-backed depending on the page extent and capacity of binding machines. Square-backs are more common in children's picture books which have little or no room to curve the spine.

There are also a number of embellishments available: **head and tail bands** lend a colourful flourish to the spine and were

originally intended to stop dust falling down the spine and cor-
roding the glue; gold **gilding** or coloured ink along one or more
edges of the book block also helps to prevent dust and moisture
slipping between the leaves; **ribbons** can be added where necessary but bear in mind that this is likely to be a manual process and
the printer will charge you for the extra time as well as materials.

EXTRA INFO AND LINKS

- Converting paper weights: https://www.papersizes.org/us-international-weights.htm; or https://www.starprintbrokers.com/resources/paper-conversion/; or https://soloprinting.com/resources/paper-weight-conversions/.

- All about head and tail bands: https://www.asiapacificoffset.com/blog_individual.aspx?bid=BLOG000084.

- The history of edge decoration and gilding: https://www.adelaide.edu.au/library/special/exhibitions/cover-to-cover/edge-decoration/.

- Embossing, gold blocking and stamping: https://www.adelaide.edu.au/library/special/exhibitions/victorian-bindings/cabinet3/.

- A number of printers, particularly larger ones in Asian countries, offer a range of weird and wonderful textured cover finishes, including holograph-foil and 'rainbow pearl' effects. Visit https://www.leo.com.hk/products-services/inspiration-gallery/empowering-your-imagination/leo-touch.html for some interesting examples.

- What are French Flaps?: https://rhollick.wordpress.com/2018/12/20/french-flaps/.

CHAPTER 15

Printing

IN A RELATIVELY SHORT time, the book printing industry has progressed from printing with slugs of metal type, inked and pressed directly onto paper, though photographic and plate-based methods, to today's high-quality digital processes. Almost everything has changed and the options are seemingly endless. However, in broad terms, and especially in the context of this book, there are only two methods you to need to know about right now: **offset** and **digital**. (Make sure you've read the previous chapter about paper and other materials before continuing.)

Offset

In the **lithographic offset** process, whole pages containing text and images are transferred either by photographic means onto thin, flexible printing plates, or 'burned' onto the plates by laser directly from a computer file (**computer-to-plate** or **CTP**). If necessary, a separate plate is produced for each of the four primary printing colours (**CMYK**) (see page 94) which, when combined, produce full colour images.

Each plate is wrapped around a cylinder and inked as it revolves. The plate is then pressed onto a revolving rubber cylinder which applies the ink to a sheet (**sheet-fed**) or a large roll (**web-offset**) of paper as it travels through the machine. The plates are usually

State of the art printing in 1568

metallic or made from a plasticised material and would wear out quickly if in direct contact with the paper, hence the *offsetting*.

Digital

This can take many forms but the most common is a hugely scaled-up form of an office laser printer where text paper is fed at high speed through a machine from a large roll. The image is taken from a computer file and applied almost magically by ink or fine powder. The paper is then cut into double-sided pages as it emerges from the end of the machine.

This method is ideal for producing small quantities of books initially and then reprints of almost any quantity. Once the text and cover files have been loaded into the machine, there are no further set-up costs in comparison to platemaking and machine *make-ready* for the offset process which, generally, have to be completed each time there is a printing. Moreover, it significantly reduces the financial 'risk' of printing a large quantity of copies

Printing both sides from a continuous roll

prior to publication. Only a small number need to be printed and stock replenished as orders are received. This is commonly referred to as **print-on-demand** or **POD** publishing.

Colour

In conventional offset printing only sheets that actually contain colour images are printed in CMYK, all other pages are printed in black ('monochrome') as usual. Colour illustrations may sometimes be grouped onto a separate set of pages and printed on gloss rather than the normal text stock. These colour sets can be inserted between sections or literally wrapped around a section to form ... wait for it ... a **wrap**.

In digital printing it is more than likely that a whole book will be run through a full colour machine, irrespective of the number of pages that contain colour images or other graphics, or where they might fall in the text.

Binding

Whichever printing method is used, the binding process starts off in basically the same way. Several pages are printed onto a sheet or roll at the same time and the order in which they are physically arranged is called the **imposition** scheme. Once printed and folded, the sheets (or segments of the roll) become **sections** (or **signatures**) containing multiples of four or eight pages (eg. either four, eight, 16 or 32 pages) ready for binding. Fairly obviously, the number of pages per section depends on the book's size relative to the sheet size — large format book pages mean fewer per sheet and therefore per section.

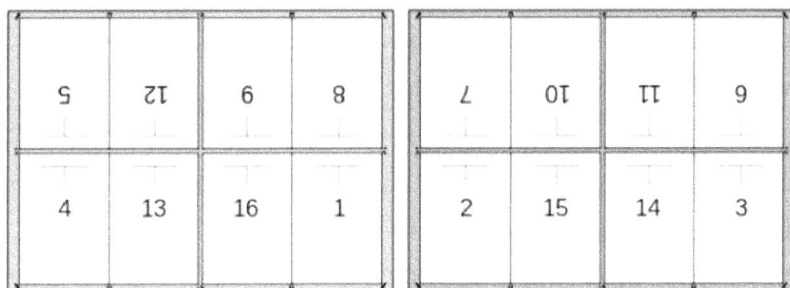

5	12	9	8		7	10	11	6
4	13	16	1		2	15	14	3

Page imposition scheme showing front and back of a single sheet

Each folded section is then added to the preceding one on a conveyor belt and gradually built up in the correct order to form a **book block**. By picking up a block and glancing at the spine, an operator can see section marks printed in successive, stepped positions on the fold to confirm that the sections are in the right position.

From here, the actual method of binding very much depends on whether the book will be paperback or hardback. For most paperback books the spine of the block is pre-trimmed using a heavy industrial guillotine to remove all folds at the spine, which then creates a perfectly flat surface with the edge of every page exposed. This, believe it or not, is called **perfect** binding because it results in a smooth, flat spine once the cover has been 'drawn on' to the block of pages and glued.

For a paperback book which will be used more robustly, such as a guidebook or a technical manual, the sections may be left folded at the spine and sewn together with thread before glue is applied and the cover added. There is a kind of compromise method where the sections are left folded but instead of sewing, notches are cut at several places along the fold to allow glue to penetrate and hold the individual pages. This is called either **burst-binding** or **notch-binding**.

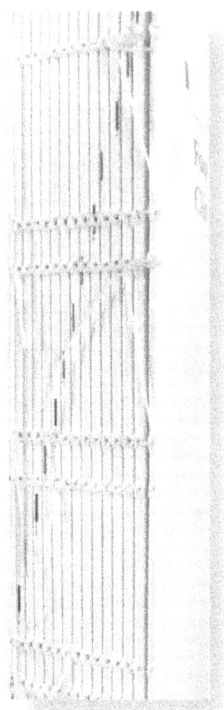

Sewn block showing step marks

The usual method of binding for hardbacks is for the sections to be sewn individually through the folded edge and then sewn together and attached to a wide strip of muslin running from top to bottom. The muslin extends past the edges of the block on both sides to form shoulders (or **super-hinges**) which are then glued to the inside of the case close to the spine and covered by the endpapers. (See the diagram on page 117)

Some hardbacks, typically children's picture books, containing only a few pages, are often glued directly onto the narrow hardback spine. This may also occur with 'blockbuster' novels, like those sold in chainstores and supermarkets, which have the outward appearance of a normal hardback (with accordingly higher retail price) but are in fact produced very much like perfectbound books with the pages glued directly onto the hardback spine.

Covers

Covers and dustjackets are produced separately from the text pages, often on presses that can print unusual or 'special' colours in addition to CMYK and apply any special coatings (eg. metallic-like inks) or varnishes (gloss or matte) in the same run.

Problems that can occur generally relate to **registration** (ensuring everything is properly aligned), possible poor conversion of colours from RGB to CMYK (see page 94) and designers not fully following instructions about trim marks or the 'safe' zone on the page layout file (see page 92).

Proofs

Printers will offer either digital proofs, sent by email, or printed paper proofs by post. It might take more time and extra expense but for covers and anything else in subtle colours I would always want to see printed proofs. There is, realistically, no other way to be sure what you see on a computer screen will be fully represented in the final printing. The way the ink sits or spreads can be quite different from the precision of a computer screen, and there may also be some unexpected differences especially if RGB colours have been converted. Check everything carefully before giving final approval — this is your last chance to get it right.

Choosing a printer

Most medium to large general printers will assure you they can produce *books*. By this they usually mean they can print the sheets that make up the pages. Whether they are capable of following through with all the remaining 'finishing' tasks of folding, collating, trimming, and binding is another matter. Some may well have the necessary equipment but, in reality, most will outsource some or all of these tasks. This may cause problems when it comes to quality assurance and, importantly, scheduling.

In particular, very few of even the largest commercial printers in Australia have their own hardback case-binding facilities and so binding is usually subcontracted to a specialist firm. As a result, your book is likely to join a long queue where it will be a one-off minnow in a large ocean dominated by big-fish publishers producing, say, thousands of hardback dictionaries or books about footy champions. Unless tightly monitored, this has serious implications for scheduling.

Printers overseas, particularly those in Asia, rarely have this problem because more often than not they have their own complete, end-to-end paperback and hardback manufacturing facilities in-house — or at least a good working relationship with an associated company.

Indeed, it is worth considering whether you should print overseas. It is not as difficult as you might imagine, especially if you use a reputable broker. They will guide you through the entire process and arrange all aspects of production for you, from checking the computer files to proofing to delivery to an Australian address. Obviously, it will take longer because of extra shipping

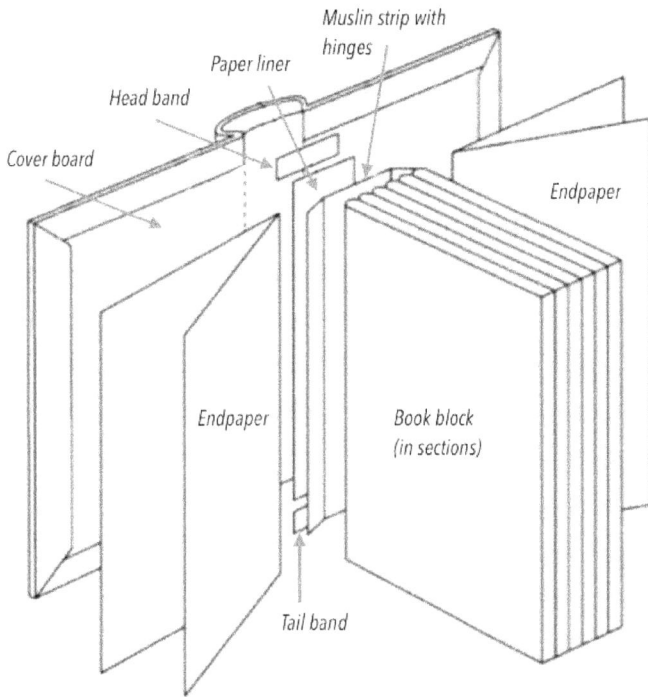

Hardback book compontents

and customs clearance (up to an additional two months) but there can be significant cost advantages. There's more in EXTRA INFO below. Also read Chapter 21 on using agents and brokers and Chapter 17 on arranging shipping from overseas.

To summarise, it is preferable to choose a printer with plenty of experience in actual *book* production rather than a general printer. To find one, you could try an Internet search for 'Australian book printer' but you are likely to just get a list of print brokers touting for work (again, see Chapter 21) and not necessarily ones in Australia either, so you might like to try one of the long-established book printers listed in EXTRA INFO as a starting point.

Quotations

To get an accurate cost quotation from a printer, you will need to provide some basic details of your project, usually by completing an online enquiry form. Bear in mind that the range of paper types and finished format sizes may be limited if you are planning to print digitally.

Book title

Copies   Total quantity required

Extent   Total number of pages including blanks

Size   Trimmed page dimensions

Format   Paperback or hardback? Portrait or landscape?

Binding   Section-sewn, notch-bound or perfect-bound?

Paperback cover   Weight and matte or gloss finish?

Case covering   Cloth or printed paper?

Printed cover   PPC and/or dust jacket?

Colour pages   Number of any sections containing full colour

Paper   Type and weight

Proofs   Digital and/or printed from plates

Advance copies   Number of copies and destination of a few copies for approval before the bulk stock is despatched

Delivery   Street address and any issues re packing or difficult vehicle access

Printers may also want confirmation that the computer files you provide for both the text pages and the cover will be to their exact PDF specifications and, if stipulated, that the page layout includes fold and trim or crop marks.

Certainly, a request for a quote *could* contain more technical details but, frankly, unless you know exactly what you're talking about, it would be better for the printer to ask specific questions and advise you accordingly. Nonetheless, they should be able to provide an accurate quote from the above specifications.

Their quote may include a provision for a small percentage of copies that can be supplied *over* or *under* the ordered amount. Standard quality control practices mean printers produce more than the required number of finished books to allow for possible spoilage. Sometimes the rejection rate is high and sometimes the opposite can happen and they have more acceptable copies than anticipated. It simply means they can deliver a slightly different amount (usually between five and 10 percent of the whole run) than ordered and charge you accordingly.

There may also be a provision in the quote (or the terms and conditions) for increases in the cost of raw materials to be passed on to the customer. For example, worldwide paper prices rose significantly during 2022-2023 and the trend continues upwards. Further, white paper is not currently being manufactured in Australia due to raw material supply issues and this has consequently increased some prices by up to 50 percent.

A printer will want you to accept their quotation as quickly as possible and their sales people may put you under some pressure to do so. For admin reasons they will want to place the project in their future schedules and budgets, so you should be absolutely clear if the quote request and the project itself are speculative and especially if you do not yet have a fixed timetable for production. Once production commences they may require you to pay part or all of the quoted amount in advance.

JOHANNES GUTENBERG AND
HIS IMPRESSIVE NEW MACHINE

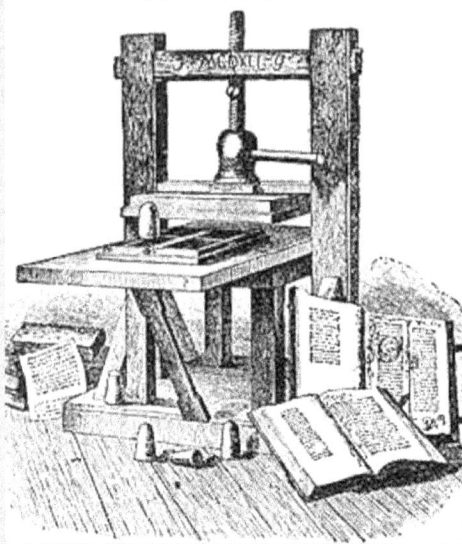

The earliest known moveable type system was created in China around 1040 firstly using baked clay and then wooden blocks. About four hundred years later, German inventor **Johannes Gutenberg** devised a mechanical printing press using reusable metal type which enabled numerous copies to be made of the same document.

This new, speedy and economical method of mass communication went on to play a major role in the Renaissance, the Reformation, the Age of Enlightenment, and greatly increased scientific knowledge throughout Europe. Gutenberg's press is now widely regarded as having had the most important impact on society in the last 1000 years.

Gutenberg's method of inked type came to be known generally as **letterpress**, and remained more or less unchanged for another five centuries until it was displaced in the mid-20th century by photo-reproduction processes, and plate or cylinder technology such as lithography and gravure.

EXTRA INFO AND LINKS

• Established Australian book printers (in 2022 all three became fully or partly owned by the OPUS Group): *(See disclaimer on p. iv)*

Ligare (Riverwood, NSW): https://www.ligare.com.au.
McPherson's (Maryborough, Victoria): https://mcphersonsprinting.com.au/AboutUs/Default.aspx.
Griffin Press (Salisbury, South Australia): https://www.griffinpress.com.au/about-us.

• Examples of overseas printers: *(See disclaimer on p. iv)*

PrintNinja is a major international print broker which sources its products from companies in China. Although its head office is in the USA it services clients worldwide via a comprehensive website and has production and logistics teams based in Shenzhen: https://printninja.com/.
KHL is a large printer in Singapore offering a wide range of services, from short-run digital to large format books in full colour: http://www.khlprint.com.sg/index.php?about-us.

• **LightningSource** is the digital printing arm of large and reputable American book distribution group **Ingram Content**. It has a branch with printing facilities in Melbourne, Victoria. Digital files are stored centrally and books can be printed off in any quantity in a number of locations around the world to fulfil orders from retail and online book-sellers including Amazon and Booktopia: https://www.ingramspark.com/. (More details on page 162)

• Brief biography of Johannes Gutenberg: https://www.britannica.com/biography/Johannes-Gutenberg.

• Stephen Fry documentary about Gutenberg and his new machine in which Fry attempts to construct a working replica: https://www.youtube.com/watch?v=uQ88yC35NjI.

CHAPTER 16

Marketing & publicity

IN THE BOOK PUBLISHING world, the term **marketing** has a wide and often confusing range of meanings but, at its most straightforward, it describes the work of presenting a product to prospective customers (the **market**) and persuading them to buy it. It might also apply to establishing and maintaining a brand (eg. *Penguin*) but this is not something that usually concerns small publishers who are typically focused on one book at a time.

Marketing can be done through free publicity, news reports, direct mail, word of mouth, social media, and by face-to-face contact with family, friends and acquaintances. Some of these activities can be passive, others can be relatively aggressive and proactive. Note that while there is some crossover, there are noticeable differences between *marketing* and some practical aspects of the *sales* function covered more fully in Chapter 18.

In setting out on the journey of publishing your book you will (hopefully) have already determined who might buy your book and have shaped it accordingly (Chapter 1). This makes the task of planning your marketing easier because you will be able to target your efforts more precisely and efficiently — and with much less effort than a scattergun approach.

Blurbs

Marketing your book starts with a basic chunk of promotional information called a **blurb**. Nobody really knows where the word came from although there have been attempts to attribute its origin to a promotion in 1906 by an author pretending to be a certain Miss Belinda Blurb. (See next page)

Conventional wisdom dictates that you need multiple blurbs of varying lengths for different purposes, such as the back cover of your book or the **Advance Information** sheet (see below), but the truth is that self-publishers need only one of about 60-80 words, plus a short paragraph about the author — and perhaps a separate line describing the contents for online bookshop purposes. In reality, no-one will read any more than one of those, wherever it appears. The generally accepted principle is that you have only a few seconds to grab a customer's attention with a cover and the blurb before they drift off elsewhere. So there's really only enough time for four or five lines.

There is a slight difference with books about specialist subjects where you need to convince a prospective purchaser that yours is better than a rival title. What is it about *your* content that beats the other guy? The best option in this situation is to include some kind of bulleted list of the key features that customers can scan quickly, followed by a line that effectively says "you should buy this book *RIGHT NOW*."

YES, this is a "BLURB"!

All the Other Publishers commit them. Why Shouldn't We?

MISS
BELINDA
BLURB

IN
THE ACT OF
BLURBING

ARE YOU A BROMIDE?

BY

GELETT BURGESS

Say! Ain't this book a 90-H. P., six-cylinder Seller? If WE do say it as shouldn't, WE consider that this man Burgess has got Henry James locked into the coal-bin, telephoning for " Information "

WE expect to sell 350 copies of this great, grand book. It has gush and go to it, it has that Certain Something which makes you want to crawl through thirty miles of dense tropical jungle and bite somebody in the neck. No hero no heroine, nothing like that for OURS, but when you've *READ* this masterpiece, you'll know what a BOOK is, and you'll sic it onto your mother-in-law, your dentist and the pale youth who dips hot-air into Little Marjorie until 4 Q. M. in the front parlour. This book has 42-carat THRILLS in it. It fairly BURBLES. Ask the man at the counter what HE thinks of it' He's seen Janice Meredith faded to a mauve magenta. He's seen BLURBS before, and he's dead wise. He'll say:

This Book is the Proud Purple Penultimate ! !

Miss Belinda Blurb demands your attention

Example of a back cover blurb:

Raising Your Pet Unicorn is the perfect guide to raising your own pet unicorn. With this handy up-to-the minute handbook you will learn to:

- Negotiate with a retail unicorn outlet
- Select the best and healthiest unicorn foal
- Build a safe enclosure in your backyard
- Plan a weekly healthy food regime
- Cook nutritious meals from scratch

If you've always wanted your very own pet unicorn, this is the ultimate guide for you and your family. It will bring you years of fun and excitement.

There should also be a short paragraph about the author. Potential customers need to know that the content is credible, authoritative and safe because the author has direct experience or expert knowledge of the subject. For example:

> Booky McBookface has studied unicornology since childhood and has successfully raised 47 unicorns from foals. She has her own 20,000 hectare rainbow farm and runs regular workshops for families who want something extra in their home life. She has a masters degree in animology from Cape Schanck University.

Advance Info sheet

Sometimes called a **New Title Information** sheet, this is a vitally important document which needs careful attention when being prepared. The bibliographic information it contains flows directly to all kinds of places so details need to be 100 percent correct. It should include:

Book cover image

Blurb

Key selling points (why someone would want to buy it)

ISBN

Format (Hb or Pb) and page extent

RRP

Type and number of illustrations

Author blurb

Details of any known media coverage

Ordering information

AI sheets are the basic tool for selling to bookshops and other retail outlets and can sometimes serve as media releases. You should consider sending printed copies, on good quality paper, rather than *en masse* by email because they may stand a better chance of being noticed. See the example AI on page 130.

Media

The most successful and long-established way to get the attention of a media outlet is to send them a **media release**. In some cases the AI can double as a release, especially if sent with a covering note. However, journalists (especially local reporters) are expected to bash out several articles every day and so the easier you can make life for them with some ready-made content, the more likely you will get their attention.

The release should contain all the relevant information about the book and be written like a standard news report itself, with quotes from the author and perhaps an expert recommendation from someone notable. The first paragraph needs to encapsulate the subject matter in an exciting way and the entire text should not be more than 300-350 words. Even if you feel your book is a bit boring, you still need to grab their attention if you want free publicity. And if you are up for it, a nice photo of the author holding or signing a copy would not go astray either.

Choose recipients of the release carefully. The obvious ones are editors of local newspapers (if you still have one in your area) but also consider other outlets such as community radio stations, regional lifestyle magazines, regional television news broadcasts, podcast hosts and, if appropriate, social media influencers. If you send a release to a statewide or national media outlet, you should try to find the name of a specific producer otherwise it will simply disappear into a general 'miscellaneous' pile of marketing guff destined for the rubbish bin.

It is debatable whether you should send a copy of the book with the release — doing so for everyone could be very expensive. However, for a select few it might just push it over the line for some positive coverage. On the other hand, please resist the temptation to call a particular reporter or broadcast producer and ask if they are going to feature your book. They absolutely do *not* like that and, ultimately, whether something appears in print or on air may not be their personal decision anyway.

If a journalist takes the bait and wants to interview you, make sure you have considered some potential questions in advance and have credible answers ready. If possible, rehearse with a mock interview with a friend beforehand.

Book launches

Launch events serve two practical purposes: first, they provide a focus for the marketing campaign and, second, they celebrate the author's awesome achievement. They also tend to be the occasion when most copies of the book are sold at any one time.

Moreover, as part of the marketing campaign, the launch is normally the key event to which members of the media are invited. Bear in mind that journalists are keen to have something on which to peg their lead paragraph (or opening comment for broadcast media) and they are looking for something that clearly fits their *who*, *what*, *where*, *when* and *why* reporting template. Having an event on which to hang a story, and perhaps take a photo or two, would obviously help things along.

The launch itself doesn't necessarily need to have an invited speaker, it can just be the author making a few comments. However, many launches do indeed have a special guest who gives a short speech, lauding the book and praising the author, and who lends some gravitas to the occasion. But don't let them ramble on and don't have more than one guest speaker.

I once attended the launch of a local history where there were *five* speakers. Yes, I know. They were the shire mayor, a former state governor, the book's publisher, the high school principal and, of course, the author himself. All of them had prepared speeches, none of which began until after the primary school band had performed a few tunes and there had been a parade of wedding dresses through the ages. I am not kidding. Please don't do that. People will leave early and they'll miss the delicious laminations prepared by the local CWA. Keep it simple and to the point.

You need to find a suitable space for the launch. It must have adequate car parking, it needs to have clear areas for people to mill around and, preferably, a raised area for the speaker(s). Be aware that once a space contains a reasonable number of people, the acoustics change as sound is absorbed so even a small area may need microphones and amplification.

Don't use a space where things can be knocked over easily or damaged (launches in art galleries are nerve-wracking) and make sure there is adequate signage if the exact location of the room is not obvious from outside the building. There is no worse PR than important guests arriving late and flustered after negotiating several lookalike corridors and doorways.

A bookshop is generally a good option for a launch because the actual task of selling books is covered by the shop so you won't have to arrange that separately. However, managers vary as to whether they will charge you for the privilege of using the shop or are prepared to just take the profits from sales on the day as their recompense. You will, of course, be expected to provide all the refreshments and nibbles.

Bookshops

Many shops have shelves dedicated to books by local authors. They will want a decent discount on the cover price as well as **consignment** or **sale-or-return** terms so they can give back any stock still unsold after a few weeks. (See Chapter 18 for more about sales.) They might take a small poster or two (see *Publicity materials* below) but it is unlikely they will put them in the front window where display space is at a premium.

Some bookshops, particularly independents, organise book clubs or online reading groups in their local area and it might be worth asking if your book could be included.

Book reviews

Timing is important if you intend to submit your book for critical review. A copy needs to go to the journal or periodical well in advance of publication so the editor can commission a reviewer who will write an article to be published around the same time as the book goes on sale. However, there is also a counter-argument that once someone has read a comprehensive review they may believe they know everything about the book and won't bother to buy an actual copy.

NEW BOOK ANNOUNCEMENT

Raising the generation our world needs

FUTURE KIND

How do we raise a generation who will effect significant positive change in our world?

And how do we effectively equip them to handle these changes, including the potential chaos they may encounter during this period of global transition?

In *Future Kind*, a unique mix of Australian academics, social commentators, educators, psychologists and writers address these questions with their own style and area of expertise. This eclectic collection of essays features themes of climate action, social justice, mental health, empathy, innovation, and sacred activism, in the context of parenting, educating, and nurturing the new generation.

Part practical guidance, personal reflection, and cultural critique, this anthology offers food for the mind and soul of parents, educators, and anyone who cares about positively impacting our future collective story.

Contributors:

Robin Grille on 'connection is resilience'

Nelly Thomas on 'feelings can be wrong'

Ricci-Jane Adams on intuitive intelligence

Phobe Mwanza on activism and allyship

Naomi Kissiedu on teaching awareness

Brigitte Kupfer on (r)evolutionary trust

Anna Lidstone on creativity and innovation

Susie Burke & Ann Sanson on realities of climate change

Marilou Coombe on leadership qualities

Andrew Lines on responsibility parenting

Rachel Forgasz on developing climate consciousness

Heidi Edmonds on parenting while saving the world

Larissa Behrendt on indigenous perspectives

Melinda Bito on connections with nature

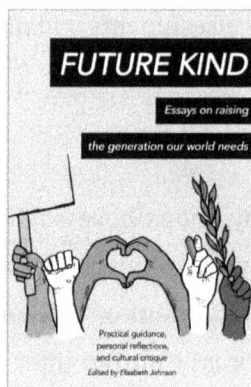

Publication 18 November 2019
Pb, 234 x 156mm, 192pp
ISBN 978-0-6487055-0-5
RRP $28.95

Promotion
Review and media copies released
in advance of publication.

**Key contributors with established
media exposure**
Nelly Thomas (books, radio and TV)
Robin Grille (books and radio)
Heidi Edmonds (radio)

Bookseller orders
Ingram Content Australia
www.ingramcontent.com/ipageaus

Published by
Radiate Publishing
enquiries@radiatepublishing.com
www.radiatepublishing.com

Media enquiries
media@radiatepublishing.com

*Example of an advance information sheet containing promotional
blurb and vital bibliographic details.
A sheet would usually also include a list of key selling points.*

You could also register your book on **GoodReads** (owned by Amazon) where it can be reviewed and given a score and perhaps prompt a few sales. Be sure to add your own author profile page so the system doesn't get you muddled up an author with a similar name. **Better Reading** is an Australian website which reviews and recommends books. Their FAQ page explains how they operate and how to submit a book to them. (See EXTRA INFO)

Social media

Posting exciting news about your book on **Facebook, X (Twitter), Instagram, TikTok (especially BookTok), Threads** or any other currently popular social media outlets, should be in two stages: first, to note that the book is coming soon, perhaps with a short extract to arouse curiosity (a kind of 'teaser') and, later, a big, bold announcement with the publication date and details of where it can be bought. Do not trigger the second stage until copies are actually available for sale otherwise it is all just a waste of time.

If you are planning to sell copies directly to customers you will need to create a **Facebook Business** page because *shopping* and *cart* functions do not currently work on personal pages (see below) EXTRA INFO has a link to research into the best times to post on social media.

Websites and Facebook

A dedicated website for your book will prove useful, especially if you want to sell copies directly to customers rather than through the bookselling wholesale and retail system. Creating a site using a **WordPress** or **Wix** template is reasonably simple but having your own domain name, with additional shopping and payment functions, will attract extra charges.

Alternatively, you could create a *Facebook* page just for your book. Again, it needs to be a *business* page so a shopping function can be added and, again, you may have to pay a monthly fee to an e-commerce provider such as **Shopify** or **BigCommerce**. (See EXTRA INFO)

Paid advertising

Advertisements need to be targeted as precisely as possible. It is important to place them in publications or on the web (eg. *Google* ads) where there is a better than 80 percent chance that potential customers will see them and react positively. Sadly, placing ads in generalist publications hardly ever works for a relatively un-known or unproven author and you may be pouring hundreds of dollars down the drain for hardly any sales benefit.

Pre-pub offer

Offering a small discount (say, 20 percent) to customers who or-der a book well before publication day can stimulate sales and is also a useful way to gauge overall interest. You will need to create a process for this, preferably via a dedicated website with a shop-ping function (as mentioned above), or you could make a mutu-ally beneficial arrangement with a local bookshop which also ac-cepts online orders. You will need to be certain of the publication date so you can tell customers when to expect their copy rather than having them hanging on indefinitely and getting increasingly annoyed with you.

Publicity materials

The design of any printed publicity materials or a website must be consistent across all elements and should definitely follow the graphic style of the cover for maximum impact. Consistency is important because it demonstrates professionalism and helps to build confidence in the content of the book itself.

It is unlikely that you will need more than a few A4 or A3 size reproductions of the front cover to use as posters in shops or at a launch. If you publicise the book in advance of its actual release you may want some smaller A5 size leaflets with the address of your own website (if you have one) and any other appropriate booksellers. If you decide to print invitations to a launch, be sure to include ordering details for those who cannot attend.

Depending on the quantities involved, PDFs can be uploaded online and printed at your nearest *Officeworks* (ideal for smaller amounts) or *Snap* shop or ordered online from *Vistaprint*. (See EXTRA INFO). You could certainly use a local independent print shop if you would prefer to support your local community but bear in mind they do tend to be more expensive.

EXTRA INFO AND LINKS

Some advice on writing a good blurb, although I don't necessarily agree with the amount of detail suggested here or indeed the total length recommended:https://blog.reedsy.com/guide/blurb/.

- A guide to the best times of the day and week to post on social media: https://buffer.com/library/best-time-to-post-on-facebook/.

- **Officeworks** printing: https://www.officeworks.com.au/shop/officeworks/storelocator.
  Snap: https://www.snap.com.au/find-a-centre.html.
  Vistaprint: https://www.vistaprint.com.au/.

- Library of free *WordPress* templates: https://wordpress.com/themes/free.

- There are a number of alternative website builders which claim to be easy to use because of their drag-and-drop capabilities. *Squarespace* is one such example: https://www.squarespace.com/.

- Info about selling through *Facebook*, with links to e-commerce providers: https://fitsmallbusiness.com/how-to-sell-on-facebook-shop/.

- Valuable advice about selling with *Facebook* ads: https://www.janefriedman.com/how-authors-can-leverage-facebook-ads-to-sell-more-books/.

- Entertaining article about a self-published author who organised an online book launch and pretended it was being streamed live from a ferry in New York: https://www.janefriedman.com/create-virtual-book-launch/.

- A highly informative book marketing website and newsletter from the UK, primarily for authors working with traditional publishers but very useful for self-publishers. Download the free booklet and subscribe to the newsletter here: https://theempoweredauthor.com/. There is also a free template for media releases at: https://theempoweredauthor.com/free-downloads-member-area.

- Book review websites include **GoodReads**: https://www.goodreads.com/; and the Australian **Better Reading**: https://www.betterreading.com.au/frequently-asked-questions/.

CHAPTER 17

Shipping & warehousing

BOOK PRINTERS, whether in Australia or overseas, will arrange delivery of books to your chosen location once they have been printed and bound. There are, however, quite a few exceptions to this general rule and there is also some industry-specific terminology you will need to get your head around.

In Australia

Printers will deliver stock using freight contractors or their own vehicles or, for small quantities (eg. using digital or print-on-demand), they may send copies by post. The printing quotation you receive may include the cost in the overall amount or it could be broken out as a separate figure. Generally, the cost rises as the distance from the print works increases.

Problems can include poor packing and stock going to the wrong location. The latter isn't just a case of getting the postcode slightly wrong. I once had a truck turn in up in a town with the same name but in a completely different state. (I mean, honestly, how many places called Griffith can there be?) So, make sure the details are unambiguously clear and correct.

Then there's the way the consignment is physically unloaded from the truck. If the delivery consists of more than a handful of boxes it is likely they will be stacked on a wooden pallet and perhaps shrink-wrapped. It is not unknown for a truck to arrive at a suburban home and the driver ask where the fork lift is. So unless you really do indeed have a fork lift tucked away in your garden shed you must specify 'no pallet unload' on the delivery instructions. Be aware that drivers don't like this because it means their valuable time is taken up with unloading manually, probably using a small trolley.

Ensuring books are packed properly and arrive in good condition is ultimately the responsibility of the printer even if the last port of call was a subcontractor such as a bookbinder. You have every right to demand that damaged stock is replaced or, more realistically, the bill is reduced.

From overseas

Overseas printers will usually arrange delivery of your books 'door-to-door' — from the printing works direct to your delivery address in Australia. In shipping terminology this is called **Carriage Insurance Freight** or **CIF**, although there are a couple of variations mentioned below.

A CIF consignment may come by airfreight if it is a small quantity but it is more likely that bulk stock will be shipped in a

Nice container ship you'e got there mister, would be a shame if it got stuck somewhere.

sea container. The printer (or perhaps an agent) will consolidate several consignments going to the same country into a container destined for a port in that country. The printer may aim to *fill* the container (**Full Container Load** or **FCL**) or take up just *part* of it (**Less than Container Load** or **LCL**). Waiting for enough products to fill or partly fill a container can add days or even weeks to the total shipping time.

Once the consignment arrives in Australia, the process of un-loading the container, gaining **customs clearance** and delivery to your chosen address will depend on the specific terms of the agreement you have with the printer. It could be included in the overall shipping cost or they may leave it up to you to arrange. You must confirm this well in advance so if necessary you can appoint a **shipping agent** who will register themselves as your agent with the relevant port authorities.

Alternatively, a printer might offer the option of delivering stock to a location in their own country on the basis that you will arrange everything from there onwards. A typical location would be the warehouse of a **freight forwarder** or shipping agent you have nominated to load and ship the consignment, collect it from the relevant port once it arrives in Australia and then deliver to your address. This is usually called **Free on Board** or **FOB**. Although this term is open to subtly different interpretations, it generally means the printing company absolves itself of any liability once delivery has been made to your specified location.

Customs, taxes and tariffs

Goods imported into Australia are liable for certain **customs duties** and taxes unless they are clearly exempt in some way. Some goods are also liable for **Goods and Services Tax** (**GST**). If you use a shipping agent they will ask you to pay any official charges before the consignment is released by **Australian Border Force** (**ABF**) officials. Trading conditions (and relevant import tariffs) between individual countries are under continual assessment by governments and conditions can change very quickly. It is always wise to check the current official situation on the ABF website (see EXTRA INFO) at the outset of your project and again during production if you planning to print overseas.

Insurance

For all the transport scenarios mentioned so far, it is vital that you confirm the physical books are fully **insured** during all stages of their journey. Check and double-check that stock is covered for loss or damage by any of the parties involved. It might be a awful thought, but it is not uncommon for containers to simply fall off ships in rough weather and be lost forever.

You should also seriously consider the importance of insurance for when copies have finally been delivered. Whether stock is under your bed, in your spare room, at the back of the garage, or stored in a commercial warehouse, there are all kinds of things that could happen without warning, especially in Australia with its often extreme weather conditions. Unless you're using print-on-demand methods, the cost of replacing even a small amount of damaged stock is probably unrealistic without insurance.

While there's nothing inherently wrong with storing books at your own residential premises (if you have the space) you should first check the provisions of your home and contents insurance policy to see if goods intended for sale are covered or how it might adversely affect your regular coverage. Otherwise you could rent a nearby commercial storage unit (or shed) through a local real estate agent and organise appropriate insurance through your usual company or agent.

Storage space

If you have persuaded a commercial book distributor to stock your book (see next chapter), delivery should be made directly to their warehouse. The only proviso would be if you need to physically sift through the books to check quality before copies go on sale. If you are not using a commercial distributor you will have to find your own storage space. Obviously this does not apply if you are publishing via print-on-demand unless the quantities you are replenishing warrant significant storage space.

In any case the area you use must be clean and dry and not subject to vagaries of the weather. Moreover, it is advisable to have some kind of barrier, such as a pallet base, between boxes and the floor to prevent any kind of moisture seeping through.

EXTRA INFO AND LINKS

- A useful glossary of shipping and freight terms: https://tauruslogistics.com.au/shipping-advice/glossary/.

- Guidance from the Australian Border Force regarding customs and taxes: https://www.abf.gov.au/importing-exporting-and-manufacturing/importing/cost-of-importing-goods.

- Australian government link to freight forwarders: https://www.austrade.gov.au/contact/faqs/how-do-i-find-a-customs-broker-or-freight-forwarder-in-australia.

CHAPTER 18

Sales & distribution

ACTUALLY GETTING your book into the hands of a purchaser is a whole other ballgame. It's the part where many new publishers trip up once copies have been printed. Yes, publicity and promotion are important and bring the title to the market's attention, but now comes the task of ensuring the book actually reaches the people it should reach.

Bricks-and-mortar

The most obvious place for your book is on display in a bookshop. By this I mean a traditional **bricks-and-mortar** shop with a big glass window, a front door and lots of shelves inside. It might be local independent store, a newsagency with a books section, or a branch of a national chain such as *Dymocks* or *Collins Booksellers* or, if your book is deemed suitable, the books section of **department discount stores** (**DDS**) like *Kmart* and *BigW*.

They need to know your book exists and where they can get copies if and when a customer orders one. The best way to do this is with an **Advance Information** sheet (mentioned in Chapter 16). Traditional publishers send sales representatives around bookshops several weeks in advance of publication to encourage pre-orders so there is no question where shops should send further orders. These reps are either employed by a single publisher or distributor or they might freelance for a number of publishers on a commission basis.

However, it is unlikely you will have the luxury of time to visit multiple bookshops yourself so sending them a hard copy of the AI is the next best thing. If you *do* decide to visit some shops, please do **not** turn up unannounced. Staff really, really don't like it, so always make an appointment.

A 1998 romcom about a small independent bookshop bullied out of existence by a new mega bookstore which undercuts them with deeply discounted prices. Ironically, in real life, a few years later an international chain of similar mega bookstores went bust arguably because they diversified into other, non-book related, products.

Start by compiling a list of all the booksellers in your immediate area and any others further afield which might have customers interested in your book. Book retailers will usually have some kind of online presence, either with their own website or at least a *Facebook* page, so a simple *Google* search should provide enough contact information for your needs. Try not to get carried away with your mailing list — postage costs might seem relatively low per item but they can soon mount up.

Another option is to place a paid-for notice in the *Weekly Book Newsletter* which serves as the publishing industry trade journal. Most bookshops subscribe to either the full version or the cut-down freebie with headlines and adverts usually emailed on Wednesdays. (See EXTRA INFO)

Whichever version of a bricks-and-mortar store you deal with, they will invariably require some kind of discount (see below) and **sale-or-return** terms if you are expecting them to take stock 'on spec.' You might be more familiar with this as 'consignment' stock but in any event it means they will take copies but only pay you when they actually sell some books. Any invoice you raise when you deliver the books should stipulate the maximum length of time they can keep the stock (usually between three and six months) before it has to be returned if still unsold.

It is, of course, entirely up to you to decide on the discount you offer a bookseller but, as a general rule, the more they want to buy, the higher the discount on offer. Currently, a self-publisher should probably be looking at offering a sale-or-return discount of somewhere between 35 percent and 55 percent off the **recommended retail price** (RRP). You also need to consider the cost of transporting books to the shop: many publishers and distributors

Try not to overpack when you despatch orders. Single books in a simple card envelope may qualify for lower postage rates especially if they are on the skinny side but for multiple copies a pre-paid post satchel may be a better option.

will add a 'small order surcharge' when the order is for just one or two copies. You must make sure the retailer is aware of all the terms when the order is placed.

The sale-or-return system is an interesting oddity of the book trade. It was introduced during the Great Depression as a short-term measure to encourage bookshops to keep ordering stock and then became an entrenched feature of the industry. It has been estimated that up to half of all books printed by traditional publishers are eventually returned; some may be put back into stock, others pulped or held for a while and then **remaindered** (see below).

Although sale-or-return certainly helps bookshops, it creates significant problems for publishers — and authors waiting for their royalty cheque — because they do not know exactly how many books have actually been 'sold-through' to paying customers until the end of the agreed return period. It also means the term 'sold out' must be treated with caution because while all of the books may well have gone out from the warehouse to shops, they could come flooding back at some point in the future.

Chainstores (ie. DDS) may want to buy **firm sale**, usually in fairly large quantities, for which they will inevitably require an equally large discount. Again, it is up to you to negotiate an appropriate rate but where there is *no* sale-or-return agreement it is common for them to demand at least 60 percent to 70 percent off the RRP so they can undercut traditional local booksellers.

Cyberselling

Selling books **online** generally comes in two distinct flavours: one that will make you the most amount of money but requires the most effort and, on the other hand, one that will make the least amount but requires the least amount of work.

By establishing your own dedicated website with e-commerce capabilities (in other words, an online shop) you will cut out any intermediaries and sell directly to your customers. (See also page 131 in the chapter on Marketing.) There is no need to apply a discount if you don't want to and, in general, books can be sold at full RRP. After deducting banking and transaction fees, plus the cost of packaging and postage, and the production cost of each book, you get to keep *everything*. This is probably the most you will make per copy sold. It will, however, necessitate physically packing individual books and multiple trips to a post office.

Alternatively, you can let established online booksellers such as *Amazon* and *Booktopia* take care of everything for you. They will want a big discount — because they supposedly sell books more cheaply than bricks-and-mortar shops — and revenue may not flow back to you for some months. If you have printed conventionally (ie. with bulk stock) you will still need to arrange to get stock to them; alternatively, if using print-on-demand, they will order copies directly from your distributor (see page 162) as and when they receive customer orders themselves.

Distributors

Unlike other countries, Australia does not have a network of large wholesalers distributing books from a wide range of publishers. In general, Australian publishers (including the local branches of multinationals) undertake their own distribution. Some may share storage facilities. They may also offer limited warehousing and distribution services to other, much smaller, usually non-rival, firms for a cut of the sales revenue. This can vary from 18 percent to 24 percent of the RRP.

There are also a number of small-scale distribution companies which will take on books from small or self-publishers, but they tend to specialise in certain subject areas and usually only accept a title for distribution if it meshes with their current 'list.'

Using a distributor will solve your warehousing issues (see Chapter 17) because, in general, they will take and hold all your books ready for distribution. However, if stock continues to sell slowly they may want to charge you for warehouse space or perhaps ask you to reduce it down to minimal 'picking' stock.

Libraries

Many self-published books, especially those that deal with local historical events, are eminently suitable for public or educational libraries. Start by finding the head office address of the regional

University and other institutional libraries will be particularly interested in history and biographical subjects.

library organisation and send a re-worded version of the AI emphasising the local angle to the *acquisitions officer*.

Libraries will typically order via the library supplier with which they already have an account but you could also try directing them to your own website (as above), perhaps with a special page and a small discount just for libraries if your e-commerce package has that kind of capability.

Stock control

If you have printed conventionally, rather than on-demand, it is important that you keep an eye on stock levels. It is very easy to sit back and plod along, merrily supplying customers and shops with copies and then suddenly find that box you thought you had at the back of the garage is not there and you have run out of copies.

Like it or not, people have become used to instant gratification when shopping online and simply don't like waiting. They will probably cancel their order if you cannot deliver in a reasonable amount of time. So make sure you have some kind of system of stock control in place to determine the pace of sales so you can order more copies from your printer in enough time. There's no need for anything sophisticated, a simple spreadsheet with comings and goings should do it.

If you have committed to paying someone else royalties you will definitely need to keep track of where and when sales are occurring so you can update your original calculations (Chapter 2) and pay them accordingly.

Remainders

Some distributors will buy 'overstock' books, commonly known as **remainders**, or perhaps more colloquially as "oh dear, we misjudged the market and printed too many" books. While you may be familiar with chains of dedicated remainder shops such as *The Book Grocer*, there are also a number of specialist companies which distribute to conventional bookshops around the country. The list in EXTRA INFO contains both kinds but it is not exhaustive and an Internet search for 'book remainders' is likely to bring up potential remainder firms in your own state.

Remaindered books are a much-debated issue, particularly in Australia, where a *lot* of 'over stock' English language books from other countries are regularly dumped. Their cheapness tends to distort the general public's perception of the average price of books, and consequently customers find it difficult to understand why new, locally published books are so seemingly expensive in comparison.

EXTRA INFO AND LINKS

- To place a notice about distribution in the publishing industry *Weekly Books Newsletter*: https://submit.booksandpublishing.com.au/?p=home/.

- A guide from the UK about getting books into High Street bookshops: https://www.societyofauthors.org/SOA/MediaLibrary/SOAWebsite/Guides/tipsforauthors0117oreilly.pdf.

- Refining and perfecting keyword searches for your book on the *Amazon* site: https://www.janefriedman.com/optimizing-books-amazon-keyword-search/. Self-publishers may also wish to consider joining the Amazon affiliates program which monitises links and referals to their fulfilment services: https://affiliate-program.amazon.com/.

- Advice from Booktopia on refining metadata to improve sales: https://www.artshub.com.au/news/career-advice/how-to-optimise-metadata-for-book-sales-2632254/.

- An interesting blog post comparing freight and shipping companies and extra charges: https://shanegowland.com/business-development/2019/aussie-delivery-services-compared-toll-australia-post-and-sendle/.

- Examples of companies dealing in remaindered books in Australia: *(See disclaimer on p. iv)*

  Castle Books: https://castlebooks.com.au/.
  The Book Grocer: https://bookgrocer.com/pages/about-us.
  BMS Wholesale: https://bmswholesale.com.au/about-us/.
  Clouston and Hall (primarily academic books): https://cloustonandhall.com.au/about-us/.

- A podcast discussing the actual events on which *You've Got Mail* is based is here: https://slate.com/podcasts/decoder-ring/2022/12/youve-got-mail-and-the-fight-between-real-bookstores.

THE PENGUIN STORY

Frustration at the dearth of inexpensive yet well designed and good quality books led British publishing executive **Allen Lane** to establish **Penguin Books** in 1935 as an imprint of his employer, The Bodley Head. Initially distributed from a church crypt, paperback Penguins became hugely popular and in 1945 the company emerged from the war years as a treasured national institution.

From the outset Lane wanted his pocket-sized Penguins to be distinctive and immediately familiar to the public and this led to simple, standardised cover designs bearing the now famous Penguin logo. They were available not only from traditional booksellers but could be found in chainstores such as Woolworths and from a innovative vending machine nicknamed the *Penguincubator*, shown above.

The company merged with US based Random House in 2013 to form Penguin Random House and the combined entity is currently one of the largest book publishers in the world. It is ultimately owned by German media conglomerate Bertlesmann.

CHAPTER 19

Legal Deposit

GOVERNMENT LEGISLATION, at federal, state and territory levels, stipulates that all publishers, whether an established mainstream publisher or a self-publisher or a club or institution of some kind, however big or small, *must* deposit at least one copy of every book title they publish with the **National Library of Australia** and with their own state library. Sometimes additional libraries are also mandated by state regulations.

While this rule applies specifically to print books and certain other items produced in physical form, the NLA and some state governments also place obligations on publishers of electronic materials. These obligations vary considerably so it is advisable to read the website for your particular state library.

The official state of publication refers to the place where you, as the publisher, have a physical presence; in other words, your street address.

When you send your book to one of the libraries listed below, you should include a covering note with the publisher's name, postal address, email address, and date of publication. You could also include a copy of the NLA CiP entry if the book does not already contain one. (See Chapter 11) Some, not all, libraries may send you an acknowledgment of receipt.

There is also a new national e-book deposit scheme: details can be accessed via the NLA website.

Australia
National Library of Australia
Legal Deposit
National Library of Australia
Canberra ACT 2600

https://www.nla.gov.au/legal-deposit/how-to-deposit

New South Wales

Legal Deposit
State Library of NSW
Macquarie Street
Sydney NSW 2000

Legal Deposit
NSW Parliamentary Library
Parliament House
Macquarie Street
Sydney NSW 2000

Gift, Legal Deposit, & Exchange
University of Sydney Library
University of Sydney NSW 2006

http://www.sl.nsw.gov.au/research-collections-building-our-collections/legal-deposit

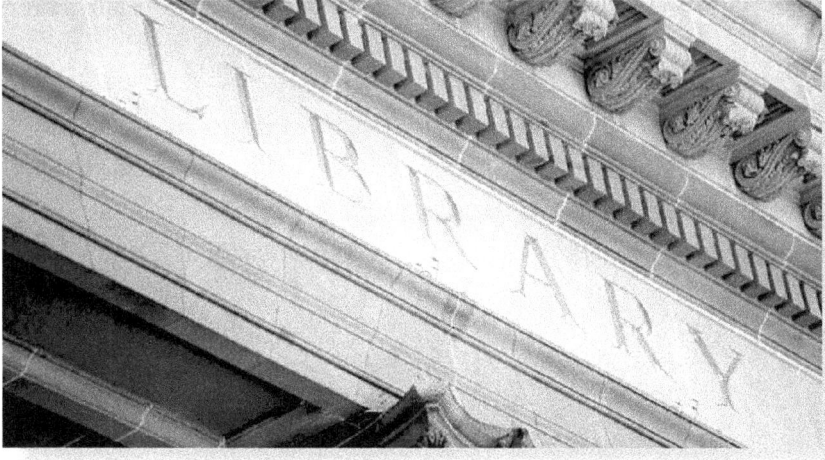

Northern Territory

Legal Deposit Team
Library & Archives NT
GPO Box 42
Darwin NT 0801

https://lant.nt.gov.au/legal-deposit

Queensland

Legal Deposit Officer
State Library of Queensland
P O Box 3488
South Brisbane QLD 4101

Parliamentary Librarian
Parliament House
George Street
Brisbane QLD 4001

https://www.slq.qld.gov.au/how-do-i/contribute-state-library-collections/
publishers-and-authors

South Australia

Legal Deposit Collection
State Library of South Australia
GPO Box 419
Adelaide SA 5001

Parliamentary Librarian
South Australian Parliament
GPO Box 572
Adelaide SA 5001

http://guides.slsa.sa.gov.au/legaldeposit

Tasmania

Legal Deposit
State Library of Tasmania
LINC Tasmania
91 Murray Street
Hobart TAS 7000

https://libraries.tas.gov.au/about-us/our-collections/tasmanian-heritage-collections/legal-deposit/

Victoria

Legal Deposit
State Library of Victoria
328 Swanston Street
Melbourne VIC 3000

https://www.slv.vic.gov.au/help/copyright-legal-deposit/legal-deposit

Western Australia

Legal Deposit
State Library of Western Australia
Perth Cultural Centre
25 Francis Street
Perth WA 6000

https://slwa.wa.gov.au/how-do-i/contribute-state-library-collections/publishers-authors

Australian Capital Territory

The ACT does not currently have a legal deposit scheme but local publishers are encouraged to lodge a copy of their work with the ACT Heritage Library.

ACT Heritage Library
PO Box 158
Canberra ACT 2601

EXTRA INFO AND LINKS

For details of the Legal Deposit scheme in New Zealand visit: http://natlib.govt.nz/publishers-and-authors/legal-deposit.

Details of the Australian e-deposit scheme: https://ned.gov.au/portal/.

CHAPTER 20

Licensing & contracts

GIVING PERMISSION to someone else to use extracts of your published work is covered in detail in Chapter 10 on copyright. To recap, you are permitting someone to reproduce part of your work for a specific purpose and accepting some 'consideration' (normally a fee) for doing so. In effect you are licensing your work for use by another person or entity. However, if your book is successful, or another publisher believes it has additional potential in a particular market, you might receive an offer to publish the whole thing commercially. In essence, it is the same deal — you are still licensing your work to someone else — but there are a few important differences.

It is completely understandable that you would be flattered by such an approach (and you probably should be after all the hard work you've put in) but you still need to be cautious in the way you respond. Commercial publishers are not charities; they will be looking to make a profit in some way, so everyone involved needs to be clear about what exactly is being proposed.

In a 'traditional' publishing setting, a publishing house or company will take the commercial **risk**. Essentially this means that in addition to royalties, they will pay all the costs associated with producing the book, from manuscript to copies delivered into the warehouse, plus marketing and distribution. Naturally, they will expect some kind of financial return on their investment.

There are several variations to this kind of author-publisher arrangement, sometimes involving a payment by the author to the publisher to underwrite a proportion of the risk. Given that you, as a self-publisher will have already put a great deal of time, effort and money into your project, this should rightly cause some hesitation on your part. Indeed, if the project is worthwhile from a commercial point of view, you should expect the publisher to be paying you royalties, not asking for a subsidy.

Contracts

As in any kind of industry, the publishing world has its own terminology, some of it quite arcane and obtuse. If you don't understand anything in a publishing contract being offered to you, don't sign it. Get advice from someone who knows what it all means. If you don't know anyone in book publishing who can help, at least get in touch with a lawyer experienced in intellectual property issues in creative industries.

A conventional book publishing contract should cover the following matters:

Parties to the agreement (the author and the publisher) and definitions and interpretation of terms used throughout.

Rights Who owns the various kinds of rights to the book or 'work'; who is being granted those rights and for what purpose and the geographic territories in which they apply; sale of subsidiary rights for a secondary purpose such as translation or dramatisation.

Author's obligations This includes completing the work by an agreed date to the publisher's satisfaction and in an acceptable format; deadlines for proofreading and making corrections; arrangements for getting outside expert opinions if necessary; guarantees about copyrights, objectionable material, libel or defamation and indemnifying the publisher accordingly; not publishing anything else that might compete; confidentiality; arrangements for possible reprints and future editions; royalties; and inspecting accounts if necessary.

Publisher's obligations Arranging to produce and publish the work; employing editors, designers and printers; consulting with the author re design and marketing; copies for the author; making the work out of print eventually; ensuring the author is identified as the author in the book and on publicity materials; paying royalties; insurances; inspection of accounts and confidentiality; arrangements if copyright is infringed by another party; termination of the agreement and reverting rights to the author.

General and other special provisions These would include arrangements for amending the agreement; which state or federal laws apply to the agreement; dispute resolution; obtaining external financial assistance (such as a grant or subsidy from a philanthropic body); any special sales arrangements; whether there is an agent for either party.

What to watch for

Without trying to pull apart or explain an entire contract, here are some key issues for a first-time author to consider:

Subsidiary rights Be careful about which rights, licence fees and royalties you allow the publisher to negotiate on your behalf and which ones you might handle yourself. This particularly applies to books that have potential for being made into movies or television series. Publishers often try to retain a large percentage of the proceeds from these kinds of sales of rights which far outweighs the actual work involved in negotiating them.

Acceptable manuscript What constitutes 'acceptable' and 'satisfactory' material needs to be carefully defined. You don't want to be in a situation of putting in a lot of extra work on your (existing) book only to find it still somehow doesn't meet the publisher's expectations.

Copyright As I have mentioned several times already, you will always retain the copyright in your work so when you sign a contract you are merely licensing someone else to use your work for a specify purpose and with a 'sunset' ending of the arrangement. Make sure the contract is clear about this.

Royalties Author groups and societies have spent many years telling members to ask for a 10 percent royalty based on the cover price. This has been, shall we say, *awkward* advice for several reasons. On the other hand, publishers may ask you to agree to a royalty based on the **nett** or **sum received** amounts without fully explaining what this actually means.

The problem arises because although publishers are obliged to recommend a retail price, they cannot control what a bookseller might *actually* sell the book for because some may discount the cover price to suit their market and, in some special cases, may actually increase the **recommended retail price (RRP)**. So publishers prefer to rely on the amount they know they will *actually* receive after all the discounts and distribution costs are taken into account.

This subject has become contentious in an era of deep discounting by chainstores and online booksellers who do not have the same kind of overheads as a High Street bookshop. To compensate, publishers may offer authors a larger royalty of 15 to 18 percent based on **nett** or **sum received** or **publisher's receipts**, all more or less the same thing. The calculations can be complex and probably require a spreadsheet to work it all out.

Creative control This is a key issue over which many authors become disappointed and frustrated with the commercial publishing process. A publisher will always consider that because *they* are taking the financial risk they should be able to decide on the final content, appearance of the book and the way the book is marketed. This may conflict with an author's vision for their precious baby. So make sure the amount of input and final decision-making is crystal clear in the agreement.

Publishing agreements can run from a four page **memorandum of understanding** (**MOU**) to a 22 page document bound with pink ribbons. Be aware that signing a contract is a serious matter and there are legal consequences if any of the parties fail to meet the stipulated requirements. Consider them carefully.

EXTRA INFO AND LINKS

- Advice on contracts from the Australian Society of Authors: https://www.asauthors.org/findananswer/contracts. The Society also publishes a book about publishing generally which contains useful advice about negotiating with traditional publishers: https://www.asauthors.org/products/asa-resources-and-guides/asas-guide-to-getting-published.

- Some Writer's Centres may be able to give advice on publishing contracts or at least point you in the right direction:

  ACT: https://marion.ink/about-marion.
  NSW: https://writingnsw.org.au/.
  Northern Territory: https://www.ntwriters.com.au.
  Queensland: https://queenslandwriters.org.au/.
  South Australia: https://writerssa.org.au/.
  Tasmania: https://taswriters.org/.
  Western Australia: https://www.writingwa.org/.
  Victoria: https://writersvictoria.org.au/.

POD AND THE INGRAM SYSTEM

The rapid growth of digital **print-on-demand** (POD) printing has given small presses and self-publishers the ability to publish books without the need for large upfront manufacturing costs. By printing books in batches of just a few copies at a time, as and when required, expenses can be tightly controlled and large stockholdings avoided.

In Australia the largest POD printer is a branch of **Lightning Source**, a division of **Ingram Content Group**, a massive, long-established American book distribution company. It has digital printing facilities in a number of locations around the world including a 50,000 square foot factory in Melbourne.

The combination of their POD operation and a well established book distribution network means that Lightning Source (known as *IngramSpark* in other countries) can offer a wide range of services in addition to printing:

- The computer files for book text and covers can be accessed for printing from any Lightning Source facility around the world.
- Retail booksellers order directly from Ingram who then print copies based on the order so there is no need for warehousing by the publisher or a distributor.
- Details of books supplied by Ingram are registered with global book databases and online bookshops such as *Booktopia* and *Amazon*.

Despite these obvious benefits, a notable downside is that the unit manufacturing cost per POD book may be higher than printing in greater quantities by other processes such as offset. Further, after discounts to retailers and distribution costs, the revenue flowing to the publisher may be only a handful of dollars per book and even then may take some months to materialise.

CHAPTER 21

Agents & packagers

THIS CHAPTER addresses issues around employing someone else to help you produce and publish your book, whether for the entire process or with some input. Note it is not about commissioning freelancers for one or two elements such as editing and design work — see Chapters 5 and 8 for more about that.

Options

While most people think of self-publishing as an entirely do-it-yourself operation, there are a growing number of alternative options available. These are generally known as **hybrid** or **assisted** forms of book publishing and can include anything from old-style **vanity** publishers to newer forms of collaborative enterprises which share the work and any potential revenue.

In an era when traditional publishers are less inclined to commission books from new or unknown writers — or at least those without a known fan base — many authors find themselves left with no choice but to organise the whole thing themselves. While they could indeed do all the work (the focus of this book) there are some firms which will publish the book under their own imprint and undertake the production and marketing work for them. Whether this is classified as *hybrid* or *assisted* very much depends on the financial details of the arrangement.

> **Hybrid** Generally an author will contribute a proportion of the production and marketing costs from their own pocket or via crowdfunding and the publisher will organise everything for them. Hybrid publishers commonly only accept manuscripts within specific subject areas because they have expertise in content, production, marketing and selling in those areas. Generally, they will work closely with the author to get the best possible outcome and then share royalties or have some other kind of revenue split with the author.

> **Assisted** This involves an author paying for a book to be produced and printed to their own specifications by a freelance agent or firm. The author retains complete creative control and owns all of the printed copies. The agent does no publicity or marketing themselves and pays no royalties. In effect, he or she manages the project or 'packages' it for a client. They may also own an imprint under which the book can be published. Such **packagers** sometimes undertake overflow production work for traditional publishers and occasionally conceptualise original projects themselves, which they then propose to publishers. Fees vary from lump sums based on the work being undertaken, to hourly rates or a percentage of major external costs such as typesetting or printing.

Whether *hybrid* or *assisted*, it is important that authors know what the total costs are likely to be and what the other party is agreeing to do. There are also issues of scheduling, especially if the company is very small or the freelancer works completely on their own and is probably juggling a number of projects at the same time.

American publishing expert Jane Friedman has an excellent chart of all the different (and shifting) publishing options which she updates annually. Definitely worth a look. (See EXTRA INFO)

Brokers

A **broker** is an intermediary who arranges a major aspect of production, such as printing overseas, on your behalf. It could be a single person based in Australia or a large web-based firm such as *PrintNinja* (mentioned in Chapter 15 on printing). Because they represent a number of clients and can guarantee plenty of work they will have negotiated a range of discounts with printers, freight companies and customs clearance agents.

Brokers will charge a percentage of the total cost as a fee. Always read the contract or agreement carefully to confirm any charges or contingency payments, or variations allowed because of changed circumstances.

Literary agents

Obviously, you don't need a literary agent to represent you if you are self-publishing. Nevertheless, there may come a point in your deliberations where you decide you would prefer to take a walk down the traditional publishing path after all. If this is the case, you should be aware that many major publishers no longer consider unsolicited submissions and will ask you to make your proposal via an agent. This is an additional filtering layer as far as the publishers are concerned. In effect, the old, traditional 'slush pile' of manuscripts waiting to be read and considered has been moved down the line. There's more about agents in EXTRA INFO.

EXTRA INFO AND LINKS

- A highly informative infographic showing the various kinds of book publishing and relationships with authors: https://www.janefriedman.com/key-book-publishing-path/.

- A good explanation of the role of an agent: https://writersvictoria.org.au/writing-life/on-writing/ask-alaa-agent-what-does-agent-do/.

- More about using an agent: https://writingnsw.org.au/support/resources-for-writers/resource-sheets/literary-agents/.

- This list of Small Press Network members contains several hybrid publishers and firms or individuals who offer various fee-based production and marketing services: https://smallpressnetwork.com.au/members/.

CHAPTER 22

Reflections

WHEN YOU SET OUT to publish your book I bet you didn't realise how much work was involved. Perhaps you arranged for others to do most of the technical stuff but, nonetheless, you successfully co-ordinated all the different elements, making decisions about design, monitoring progress and organised marketing. That, in itself, is a huge achievement, so give yourself a big high five.

Now it's time to sit back a little and consider how it all went. This is an especially valuable exercise if you want to produce and publish more books in the future. Ask yourself some pertinent questions and note the answers for future reference:

- Is the final result (the printed book) exactly as you envisaged it? If not, what changed and why?
- Was the design you chose the best option? If not, what would have been better?
- Did it take as long as you originally calculated? If not, what could you have done to change the schedule?

- Was the final total cost the same as your original estimate? Which costs blew out and where did you save money?
- How good was the relationship with any freelancers you used? Did they keep to budget and the schedule?
- Could you do any outsourced elements yourself next time?
- Did the publicity and marketing strategy work? How could it have been improved?
- Have strategies for sales and distribution been successful? Could they be improved further?
- What do you feel you have learned about the publishing process overall?
- Would you do it again (be honest!)?

Reviews

There will, of course, be *others* who will read and perhaps write a review or pass comment on your book. They may not as kind as your family in what they say about it. Don't let it get to you. It's just their *opinion*, probably based on how *they* would have done it. But they didn't do it. You did. Be proud of your achievement.

CHAPTER 23

Checklists

THE FOLLOWING PAGES contain, first, a checklist of the main stages in producing a printed book and, second, a list of the potential costs. All elements have all been mentioned in previous chapters.

Feel free to expand the production list or otherwise add tasks as you wish. For example, under *Editing* you may wish to add chapters or parts of your book to tick off when they have been completed; under *Illustrations* you may want to include a check to confirm images have been scanned correctly. You may also find it useful to add deadlines and other relevant information.

Use whatever method of day-to-day project management is best for you and which helps keep everything on track; some people like to use a printed diary to log progress and set deadlines. It can also be useful to include reminders a few days in advance of actual deadlines. If you do use a diary, it is always wise to make entries in pencil because a single missed deadline will probably mean you have to move and rewrite all the subsequent entries.

BASIC PRODUCTION CHECKLIST

Pre-Production

Primary tasks

- ☐ Establish concept
- ☐ Scoping and estimating
- ☐ Writing
- ☐ Illustrations, photos, permissions
- ☐ Editing
- ☐ Gather all material

Secondary tasks

- ☐ Business registrations: ATO, ASIC
- ☐ Obtain ISBNs and barcodes
- ☐ Seek funding

Production

Primary tasks

- ☐ Text and cover design
- ☐ Typesetting and layout
- ☐ E-book formatting
- ☐ Indexing
- ☐ Proofreading
- ☐ Final print quotes
- ☐ Upload files for print, e-book
- ☐ Proofing

Secondary tasks

- ☐ Apply for CAL, PLR, ELR, NLA entry
- ☐ Establish e-book sales channels
- ☐ Pre-marketing: media releases etc.

Post-production

Primary tasks

- ☐ Marketing and publicity
- ☐ Warehousing

- ☐ Distribution
- ☐ Legal deposit
- ☐ Launch
- ☐ Reviews
- ☐ Sales and despatch

Secondary tasks

- ☐ Selling rights
- ☐ Remaindering

POTENTIAL EXPENSES

- Business name registration
- New publisher registration
- ISBNs, barcodes
- Manuscript assessment
- Freelance photographer
- Illustration, photo permission fees
- Freelance copyeditor
- Page layout software
- Freelance designer
- Freelance typesetter
- Printing page proofs
- Freelance indexer
- Uploading files for print, e-book
- Internet domain name
- Premium website template
- Online e-shop fees
- Printing and posting media releases, trade info
- Advertising
- Printing final copies
- Shipping, freight, customs fees
- Launch event
- Printing and posting review, legal deposit copies

Index

www.ingramcontent.com/pod-product-compliance
Lightning Source LLC
Chambersburg PA
CBHW072132020426
42334CB00018B/1773